MARRIAGE BONDS
and
MINISTERS' RETURNS
of
HALIFAX COUNTY, VIRGINIA
1753–1800

COMPILED AND PUBLISHED
by
CATHERINE LINDSAY KNORR
1957

This volume was reproduced from
an 1957 edition located in the
publishers private library
Greenville, South Carolina

Please direct all Correspondence & Orders to:

Southern Historical Press, Inc.
P.O. Box 1267
375 W Broad Street
Greenville, S.C. 29602-1267

Originally published & Copyrighted:
            Catherine Lindsay Knorr 1957
Copyright Transfered: Southern Historical Press, Inc. 1982
ISBN: 978-0-89308-259-8
Printed in the United States of America

To

Edward Boyd Vinson

and his sweet wife

Myra June (Burris) Vinson

who have published nine

books for me and by

their inexhaustible patience,

cheerful co-operation and

unbelievable efficiency have

taken out all the woes

of book-making and left me only

the happiest of memories.

```
                    CHARLES CITY
                        1634
                        │
                  PRINCE GEORGE
                        1703
                        │
        ┌───────────────┴───────┐           ┌───────────┬───────────┐
    BRUNSWICK                                AMELIA              DINWIDDIE
      1732                                    1735                 1752
        │                                       │                   │
  ┌─────┴──────┬────────┬──────────┐    GREENSVILLE  PRINCE EDWARD  NOTTOWAY
LUNENBURG                         1781         1754           1789
  1746
  │      │          │          │
HALIFAX  BEDFORD  CHARLOTTE  MECKLENBURG
 1752     1754      1765       1765
```

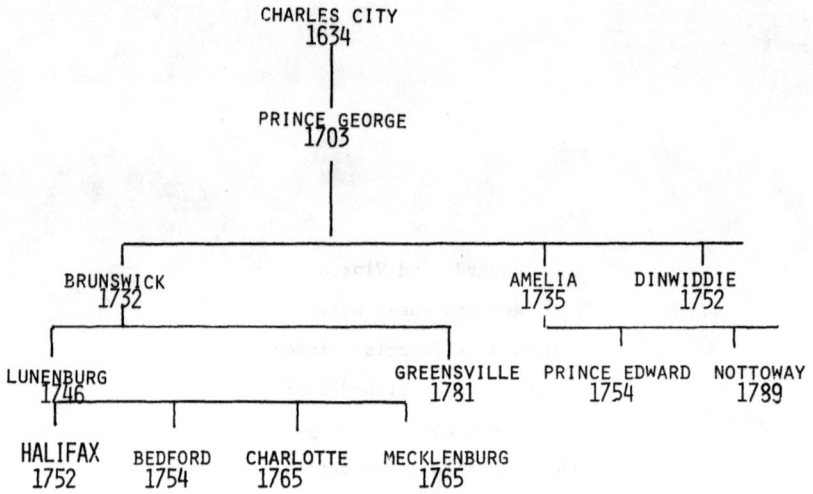

(ROBINSON P. 164 CHART NO. 2)

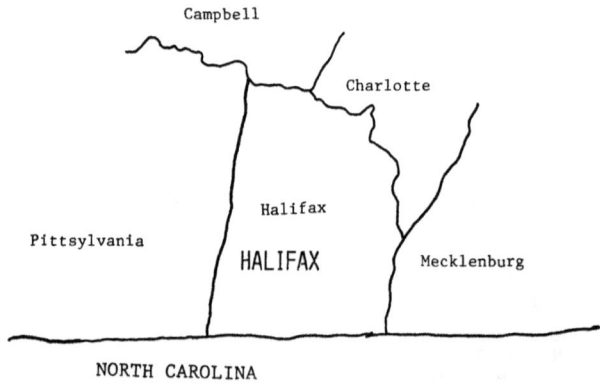

```
                    Campbell

                              Charlotte

                        Halifax

Pittsylvania
                        HALIFAX        Mecklenburg

        NORTH CAROLINA
```

Publisher's Preface

Mrs. Knorr died in 1975, and after her death these books of marriage records were kept in print and sold by her late husband. Upon his death, they became the property of her grandson, Hal Wyche Greer, III, of Marietta, Georgia, who continued to sell them on a limited basis.

In mid-1981 I sought to find Mr. Greer to discuss with him the possibility of obtaining the exclusive publishing and sales rights to these 14 titles. In due time, Mr. Greer and I were able to negotiate a contract for my exclusive sales and publication rights to these books. It was agreed that Mr. Greer would have a final voice on the changing of the format of any of these titles when they needed to be reprinted. I suggested to Mr. Greer that when these various books sold out and a reprinting had to be done, that for the sake of cost, I would publish them in a 6" x 9" page size, but that the format and style would remain the same, and this was agreed upon.

The reader is cautioned to note that these new 6 x 9 pages are typed verbatum from Mrs. Knorr's original copy, and page by page, so that new indexing was not required. It was also decided that when a book went out of print, it would be retyped on an electric typewriter with a carbon ribbon for better legibility. As publisher, I felt it was important to call to the attention of the reader these changes and the reason for eventually bringing out all of these titles in a 6 x 9 book.

The Rev. S. Emmett Lucas, Jr.
Publisher

Preface

Virginia named thirteen of her counties after prominent Englishmen of which Halifax was one. It was named in honor of George Montague 2nd Earl of Halifax who was the First Lord of the Board of Trade about that time and as such greatly interested himself in the trade with the Colonies. George Montague, born 6 October 1716, Viscount Sunbury till 1739 when he inherited the Earldom of Halifax died 8 June 1771 at the age of fifty-four. (C. P. (2) VI 247-248).

The new county was formed from Lunenburg, the separation taking place 17 April 1752. The territory at that time included the present Pittsylvania, Henry and Patrick counties.

The first court was held at the home of Hampton Wade on the 17th Day of May 1752. Gentlemen Justices present were: William Byrd, William Wynne, Peter Fontaine, Jr., James Terry, William Irby, Nathaniel Terry, Robert Wade, Hampton Wade, Andrew Wade, Hugh Moore and Sherwood Walton. Nathaniel Terry was the first Sheriff and the first Clerk of the Court was George Currie. Thomas Nash was appointed surveyor.

John Bates and William Harris represented the new county of Halifax as the first Burgesses. They sat in the 1st November 1753 session of the House of Burgessess.

After George Currie, who was Clerk 1752-1757, the following gentlemen held that office: Robert Munford, Paul Carrington, George Carrington and John Wimbish whose term of office ran well into the 19th century. Henry Goare who witnessed so many of the marriages in this book was Duputy Clerk from 1776 to 1792.

Antrim Parish of the Episcopal Church is nearly as old as the county. The Vestry record book 1752 - 1818 is in the Court House. "At a Vestry held for Antrim Parish in Halifax County on Wednesday XVIth day of July 1752: Present, James Terry, Richard Echolls, Thomas Dillard, Thomas Calloway, Ricard Brown, William Irby, Merry Webb, Peter Wilson, William Wynne, John Guillingtine and John Owen.

"Ordered that the several Readers in this Parish who were appointed by the Vestry of the Parish of Cumberland in the County of Lunenburg be continued in their respective places till the laying   of the Parish levy which is supposed or intended to be on the XVIIth day of October next.

John Owen and Thomas Calloway are appointed church wardens of this Parish for the ensuing year.

"John Cook is appointed Clerk of this Vestry and it is ordered that he continue in that office until the laying of the Parish Levy."

And nothing further appearing before them they adjourned. The minutes of these preceedings were signed: "Truly recorded, Teste: William Wright, Clerk for the Vestry."

Modern Halifax is delightful. The mellow old Court House is flanked on three sides by charming brick houses, two room, one storied houses that are the offices of the Halifax attorneys. I believe they are the property of the county and assigned to the lawyers. At any rate, it is a practical arrangement, designed to keep smart young Halifax lawyers in Halifax.

Many of the magnificent old homes are still standing and when I could get my nose out of the fascinating records I loved to ride around the town and county to marvel at their wonderful state of preservation and the groomed look of their grounds.

In front of every business house in Halifax all up and down each side of Main Street is a blue tub. And guess what's growing in each tub! A stalk of tobacco advertising the county's main crop. Watered and tended like rare plants they grow to prodigious heights and flower, too, just to reward their owners; great spikes of lovely pale pink blossoms.

Mr. H. M. Sizemore, the Clerk of Halifax, is just what a County Clerk should be, amiable, helpful, thoroughly conversant with the records and the soul of courtesy. His deputies enhance the pattern he sets by being about the most co-operative people a court house was ever blessed with, creating an atmosphere of good will that felt just like Christmas! When I'd feel hurried and work through the noon hour, Dorothy Clements or Cornelia Conner would bring me my lunch. Tobacco isn't all that flowers in Halifax.

Everybody is nice. When I stepped on what was probably the only loose lid on a Halifax water meter, Dr. Nathaniel H. Wooding took beautiful care of my wrenched foot and taped it up so I could drive two days later. In him I discovered a kindred spirit and a student of Virginia history.

Mrs. Day, my landlady, made my several stays in Halifax just as pleasant as they could possibly be made with such extra curricular services as chauffeur and guide to historic spots.

Since no modern Court House is staffed to answer letters of inquiry requiring research, those who want to delve in Halifax are fortunate to have Mrs. Berryman Green, who lives fives miles south in New Boston. It was she who checked for me all the pages of discrepancies that appeared.

Mrs. Green, a genealogist thoroughly conversant with Halifax names and families, can and will search the wills and deeds should you desire further information. Her address is: Mrs. Berryman Green, 101 Broad Street, South Boston, Virginia. I'm sorry I can't do it for you myself because I'd love an excuse to go back, but it's a comfortable feeling for me to leave you, my good friends, in her capable hands.

Catherine Lindsay Knorr

MARRIAGES OF HALIFAX COUNTY, VIRGINIA
1753 - 1800

23 May 1797. Armistead ABBOTT and Frances Priddy, dau. George Priddy who consents. Sur. James Priddy. Wit. Lewis Priddy. p 36

29 October 1793. Elisha ABBOTT and Lydda Clay, dau. Margaret Clay who consents. Sur. James Clay. Wit. Hopkins Muse. Marriage by Rev. Hawkins Landrum. p 28

19 December 1799. Jacob ABBOTT and Polly Dickson. Married by Rev. Hawkins Landrum. Ministers' Returns p 145

26 December 1796. Joseph ABBOTT and Elizabeth Priddy, dau. George Priddy who consents. Sur. William Goodwin. p 35

26 December 1787. Matthew ABBOTT and Sarah Casady. Sur. William Casady. Sarah signs her own consent· p 11

1 December 1798. David ABERNATHY and Lavenia Townes, dau. Lucy Townes who consents. Sur. Isaac Oliver. Wit. Stephen Stuart. (Was she a dau. of Stephen Townes who married Lucy Watkins 2 October 1777?). Married 18 December by Rev. James Watkins. p 40

15 June 1786. Reubin ABNEY and _____ Petty. Sur. William Cole. p 8

21 December 1795. James ADAMS and Elizabeth McGriger, dau. John McGriger who consents. Sur. James Preston. Wit. John McGriger, Jr. and Daniel McGriger. Married by Rev. Samuel D. Brame. p 32

25 August 1800. James M. ADAMS and Rachel Hands. Sur. John Jones. Wit. Joseph Jones. Rachel signs her own consent. Married by Rev. Hawkins Landrum who says Handy. p 44

27 October 1781. John ADAMS and Mary Thompson, dau. John Thompson. Sur. Joseph Prewitt. Wit. Byrd Prewitt and Robert Prewitt. Married by Rev. Nathaniel Hall. p 5

31 August 1791. John ADAMS and Prudence Thornton. Sur. Samuel Hubbard Prudence signs her own consent. p 20

24 September 1799. Joseph ADAMS and Elizabeth Wadkins. Sur. Fleming Bridgeman. Elizabeth signs her own consent. p 42

20 June 1797. Moza ADAMS and Polley George, dau. Johnadab George who consents. Sur. Ramsey Booker. Wit. James Hunt, John Martain and Samuel Hubbard. p 36

1

13 September 1785. Nipper ADAMS, Jr. and Polly Farmer. Sur. Samuel Whitehead. Wits. William Price, Robert D. Milner and Enoch Farmer. Nipper is son of Nipper Adams, Sr. Married by Rev. William Dodson. Returns in December. p 7

26 May 1791. Nipper ADAMS and Obedience Farmer. Sur. Nathaniel Mannin. Consent of Frederick Farmer for Obedience; no relationship stated. Married 16 June by Rev. Hawkins Landrum. p 20

22 June 1795. Nipper ADAMS and Frances Carter. Sur. John Anderson. Wit. Richard Carter. Frances signs her own consent. Married 1 July by Rev. Hawkins Landrum. p 32

16 August 1781. Richard ADAMS and Elizabeth Prewet. Married by Rev. Nathaniel Hall. Ministers' Returns p 204

2 February 1792. Sylvester ADAMS and Rebekah Boyd. Sur. William Thaxton. Rebekah signs her own consent. Married 9 February by Rev. Reuben Pickett who says Rebecca. p 26

11 November 1782. Thomas ADAMS and Rachel Nobles. Married by Rev. Nathaniel Hall. Ministers' Returns p 206

23 January 1796. John ADKINS and Ginsey Lumkin, dau. Ann Lumkin who consents. Sur. William Ryan. Wit. William Atkins. p 35

13 October 1789. Robert ADKINS and Nancy Battell. Married by Rev. Reuben Pickett. Ministers' Returns p 46

24 December 1788. William ADKINS and Isbell Boyd. Sur. James Boyd. Married 30 December by Rev. Reuben Pickett. p 14

15 December 1800. Harrison AKIN and Patsey Johnson, dau. James Johnson who consents. Sur. Isham Palmer. Wit. Armistead Akin, Aaron Hardwick, Isham and Sally Palmer. Edward Akin, father of Harrison consents for him. Married by Rev. John Atkinson. p 45

28 July 1800. James AKIN, Jr. and Lucretia Townes, dau. Lucy Townes who consents. Sur. David Abernathy. Married 5 August by Rev. James Watkins. p 44

30 October 1794. Robert AKIN and Polley Graves, dau. James Graves who consents. Sur. John Fallis. See Robert Atkin. p 29

14 December 1795. William ALDERSON and Sally Hitson. Sur. William Cole. Sally signs her own consent. Married by Rev. William Moore. p 32

22 October 1793. Abner ALLEN and Polly Dejarnett. Sur. Richard Allen. Polly signs her own consent. Married 24 October by Rev. Hawkins Landrum. p 28

30 October 1797. Charles ALLEN and Elizabeth Powell. Sur. Marston Powell. Wit. Robert Wooding. Elizabeth signs her own consent. Marstan also written Mastin on bond. Married 1 November by Rev. Leonard Baker. p 36

29 April 1783. David ALLEN and Apphia Lewis. Sur. John Lewis, Sr. Wit. Henry Goare. p 6

29 May 1797. David ALLEN and Anne Owen. Sur. Benjamin Conner. Wit. Elisha Palmer. Anne signs her own consent. Married 31 May by Rev. Thomas Dobson. p 36

28 September 1795. William ALLEN and Susanna Elizabeth Echols. Sur. John Echols. Susanna signs her own consent. Married 3 October by Rev. Hawkins Landrum. p 32

23 December 1800. William ALLEN and Aney Sims. Sur. Matthew Sims. p 44

26 January 1795. John ANDERSON and Sarah Pettey. Sur. Joseph Pettey. p 32

26 December 1791. Thomas ANDERSON and Polley Haley. Sur. Obadiah Kerby. Wit. Joseph E. Haley and Frankey Haley. Married 5 January 1792 by Rev. James Watkins.

25 June 1798. Benjamin ANDERTON and Sussanna Roberts. Sur. Moses Roberts. p 40

21 June 1780. George ANDERTON and Molley Roberts. Sur. Robert Wooding. Wit. Betty Roberts, Sally Roberts and William Roberts. Molley signs her own consent. p 4

19 August 1784. Alexander ANDREWS and Susanna Vaughan. Married by Rev. Nathaniel Hall. Ministers' Returns p 7

        1790. Samuel ANNATT and Eliza Johnson. Married by Rev. John Atkinson. See Samuel Aunatt. Ministers' Returns p 48

1 January 1759. John ARMSTRONG and Margaret Boyd (widow). Sur. Alexander Irwin. Wit. William Wright. p 1

21 December 1786. David ARNOLD and Cuzza Mitchell. Sur. William Arnold. Married 23 December by Rev. Thomas Dobson who says Cuzakiah. p 10

11 January 1790. David ARNOLD and Maryan Carter. Sur. Robert Cole. Robert Carter consents for Maryan; no relationship stated. Married 14 January by Rev. Hawkins Landrum. p 17

17 August 1787. William ARNOLD and Elizabeth Noell. Sur. Garnett Noell. Wit. Thomas Noell and Drusillar Noell. Elizabeth signs her own consent. p 11

28 January 1799. Benjamin ARRINGTON and Fanny Hunt. Married by Rev. Hawkins Landrum. Ministers' Returns p 143

23 September 1795. Mical ASBRUCK and Ruth Wilson. Married by Rev. William Moore. Ministers' Returns p 116

7 November 1785. William ASHLOCK and Sarah Sullins, dau. Nathan Sullins. Sur. John Sullins. p 8

30 August 1790. William ASHLOCK and Sarah Coneley, dau. William Coneley who consents. Sur. Thomas Brown. Wit. William Thompson. Married 2 September by Rev. Hawkins Landrum who says Connelly. p 17

6 September 1795. John ASKEW and Polley Rhodes. Sur. Barnard Harris. Wit. Nathaniel Vasser. Polley signs her own consent. p 31

13 November 1795. John ATKERSON and Sally Watkins. Sur. James Watkins. Married 19 November by Rev. Reuben Pickett. p 32

30 October 1794. Robert ATKIN and Polly Graves. Married by Rev. John ATKINSON. See Robert Akin. Ministers' Returns p 97

14 October 1800. John ATKINSON and Sarah Pickett. Sur. Obadiah Roberts. Wit. Susanna Pickett. Sarah signs her own consent. p 44

22 June 1789. Josiah ATKINSON and Susannah Wall. Sur. Charles Wall. Married by Rev. Atkinson. p 15

28 October 1799. Thomas ATKINSON and Rachel Link, dau. Barton Link, who consents. Sur. Clement Tranum (Traynham). Wit. Jesse Atkinson. Married 7 November by Rev. Reuben Pickett. p 41

15 December 1799. Jesse ATKISSON and Jinney Medley, dau. James Medley who consents. Married by Rev. Reuben Pickett who says Atkinson. p 42

14 October 1790. Samuel AUNATT and Elizabeth Johnson, dau. Joseph Johnson who consents. Sur. John Covington. Wit. James McKenny. See Samuel Annatt. p 17

13 February 1786. Elisha AYRES and Lidda Owen, dau. John Owen. Sur. William Peter Martin. p 8

29 March 1794. Joseph Murphy AYRES and Leanner Owen, dau. John Owen who consents. Sur. Christopher Russell. This name is spelled Ayers also Aeyrs. p 29

December 1783. Ezekiel BAILEY and Peggy Bradley, dau. James and Peggy Bradley who consent. Wit. William Scales. Consent only. p 6

15 December 1785. Ezekiel BAILEY and Peggy Bradley. Sur. Robert Williams. p 7

12 February 1788. Thomas BAILEY and Elizabeth Stone. Sur. John Stone. p 14

12 November 1789. James BAIRD and Sarah Wade. Sur. John Boyd. Wit. Mount Plisent and William Tomson. Both James and Sarah sign their own consents. Married by Rev. Reuben Pickett. p 15

14 November 1787. Leonard BAKER and Frances Street. Sur. William Hall. p 10

13 November 1798. Richard BALL and Susanna Adams. Sur. Samuel Crawford. Wit. John Adams, Sr. Susanna signs her own consent. p 40

16 December 1793. Edward BALLINGER and Nancy Edwards. Sur. Benjamin Edwards. Married by Rev. John Atkinson. p 28

25 December 1800. Shadrock BARBER and Salley Winfree, dau. Charles Winfree who consents. Sur. Thomas Jines. Wit. Jacob Amonett. p 44

30 September 1800. Beverly BARKSDALE and Judy Womack. Sur. Achilles Whitlock. Wit. John Womack. Consent of Charles Womack for Judy; no relationship stated. Married by Rev. John Atkinson. p 43

11 January 1781. Peter BARKSDALE and Elizabeth Watlington. Sur. Samuel Marvin. Wit. Henry Goare. Armistead Watlington signs consent; no relationship stated. His will Book 7, p 322 dated 2 November 1803 pro. 22 June 1807 mentions dau. Betsy Barksdale and son-in-law Peter Barksdale. p 5

23 October 1797. John BARLEY and Melley Sneed. Sur. Evan Sneed. p 36

17 August 1786. Jesse BARNES and Elizabeth Jones, dau. Anne Jones who consents. Sur. Henry Barnes. Wit. Richard Tankersley and John Jones. p 10

6 March 1788. Charles BARTLETT and Catey Rogers. Sur. Joseph May. Married 9 March by Rev. Reubin Pickett. p 14

29 September 1779. James BARTLETT and Tempey Whitlock. Sur. John Banks. Wit. John Bartlett and James Smith. Tempey signs her own consent. p 4

20 October 1800. Peter BASS and Jane Carr. Sur. William Carr. p 44

21 December 1789. William BASS and Rachel King, dau. Henry King who consents. Sur. Daniel Easley. Wit. Isaac Easley. p 15

27 July 1789. Charles BATES and Mary Martin, dau. William Martin who consents. Sur. Daniel Bates. Wit. John Martin. p 15

25 February 1782. Daniel BATES and Jane Snelson, dau. Charles Snelson. Sur. Peter Barksdale. Wit. Stephen Bates. p 5

2 February 1782. David BATES and Drusilla Echols. Sur. Moses Echols. Wit. Henry Goare. p 6

8 September 1791. Fleming BATES and Peggy Milliner. Sur. Presley Dodson. Married by Rev. John Atkinson. p 21

31 March 1788. James BATES and Susan Wirt. Sur. Presley Dodson. p 12

20 January 1793. James BATES and Levina F. Nance. Sur. William H. Hunt. Levina signs her own consent. p 28

11 August 1792. Matthew BATES and Judah Earle. Sur. Presley Dodson. Married by Rev. John Atkinson. p 25

1 September 1790. Samuel BATES and Biddy East. Sur. Daniel Bates. Biddy signs her own consent. p 20

5 February 1793. William BARNES and Rebeckah Munford. Sur. Fielder Cage. Nancy Muentford consents for Rebeckah; no relationship stated. She spells it Muntford. Married by Rev. Hawkins Landrum. p 29

6 January 1795. John BAYNES and Sally Colquett. Sur. Benjamin Davis. Wit. Robert Akin. Sally signs her own consent. Married by Rev. John Atkinson. p 32

22 March 1757. Joseph BAYS and Ann Robertson. Sur. John Robertson. Wit. William Wright. p 1

28 November 1782. John BEAL and Rebecca Bays. Married by Rev. Nathaniel Hall. Ministers' Returns p 210

2 March 1785. William BEAL and Betsy Murphy. Sur. William Murphy. Wit. Henry Goare. p 7

2 May 1787. David BELL and Frances Gent. Sur. Garnett Noell. Wit. Skearn Osborn. Frances signs her own consent. p 12

9 November 1793. John Ellis BENTLEY and Kaziah Younger, dau. William Younger who consents. Sur. Samuel Bentley. Married 13 November by Rev. Leonard Baker. p 27

25 September 1795. Samuel BENTLEY and Nancy Le Grand, dau. John Le Grand who consents. Sur. Orvill Tunstall. Wit. Elizabeth Gunn. p 32

25 January 1796. William BENTLEY and Nancy Wills. Sur. John Murphy. Nancy signs her own consent. Married 27 January by Rev. Hawkins Landrum. p 34

4 August 1795. Thomas BEST and Sally Long. Sur. Henry Thomas, Jr. Wit. Thomas Puckett. Sally signs her own consent. p 33

26 November 1798. Nathan BETTERTON and Edna De Jarnett, dau. M. De Jarnett (father) who consents. Sur. John Wimbish. Wit. Charles Sydnor. p 41

30 April 1788. Matthew BILBO and Edna George, dau. John George who consents. Sur. William Terry. William Shelton and Nathaniel Bowman. p 13

8 May 1782. John BIRCHFIELD and Elizabeth Hendrick. Married by Rev. Nathaniel Hall. Ministers' Returns p 9

25 January 1790. Tarlton BLACK and Elizabeth Owen. Sur. Richard Owen. Married 11 February by Rev. James Watkins. p 20

12 September 1788. William BLACK and Nancy Hawkins. Consent of Joseph Collins, guardian of Nancy. Sur. Stith Harrison. p 12

9 October 1799. James BLACKWELL and Elizabeth McCarty. Married by Rev. Reuben Pickett. Ministers' Returns p 137

2 January 1786. Moses BLACKWELL and Suckey Wall. Sur. George Wall. p 10

19 October 1797. Robert BLACKWELL and Charity Stone. Sur. Joshua Powell. Married by Rev. Leonard Baker. p 36

11 July 1787. William BLACKWELL and Mary McCarty. Sur. Charles McCarty. Wit. John Watson and Robert Childers. Mary signs her own consent. Married 14 July by Rev. Reuben Pickett. p 10

25 December 1800. William BLANE and Nancy Faulkner. Sur. Daniel Collins. Wit. Isaac Coles. Married by Rev. Reuben Pickett. p 44

21 March 1791. Joseph BLANKS and Frankey Jones. Married by Rev. Jesse Owen. Ministers' Returns p 60

10 January 1782. William BLANKS and Marian Robertson. Married by Rev. Nathaniel Hall. Ministers' Returns p 206

15 March 1797. John BOHANNON and Susanna Yates. Sur. William Yates. Consent of Francis and Ann Yates for Susanna; no relationship stated. Susanna also signs the certificate. Married 17 March by Rev. William Moore. p 36

2 January 1800. Armistead BOMAR and Betsy Younger. Married by Rev. Hawkins Landrum. Ministers' Returns p 145

7 February 1780. John BOND and Susanna Wade, dau. Stephen Wade. Sur. John Harvey. Wit. Henry Goare. p 4

30 May 1789. Edward BONNAR and Mary Wood. Sur. John Wood. p 17

8 July 1800. James BOOKER and Susannah Price, dau. Daniel Price who consents. Sur. Richard Booker. p 44

4 April 1770. Parham BOOKER and Frances Martin. Sur. Thomas Yuille, Gent. Wit. William Wright. p 2

2 November 1770. Richard BOOKER and Elizabeth Palmer, dau. John Palmer. Sur. George Murdock. Wit. William Wright. Thomas Yuille, Gent. signs the certificate for Richard Booker. p 2

2 October 1788. Richard BOOKER and Elizabeth Moore. Consent of John Moore for Elizabeth; no relationship stated. Sur. John Watlington. Married 6 October by Rev. John Atkinson who says Richard E. Booker. p 13

15 December 1785. Shields BOOKER and Anne Pride, dau. William Pride. Sur. H. or N. Townes. Wit. George Carrington. p 6

19 December 1795. Thomas P. BOOKER and Fanny Terrell. Sur. John Carter. p 33

10 October 1785. Frederick BOOTT and Elizabeth Comer. Married by Rev. Thomas Dobson. See Frederick Bott.

4 February 1783. George BORIUM and Peggy Murphy. Sur. William Murphy. Wit. Henry Goare. p 6

17 January 1788. John BORUM and Judith Hendrick. Sur. Moses Hendrick. Wit. John Anderson. Married by Rev. William P. Martin. p 13

6 June 1762. Absalom BOSTICK and Bethenia Perkins. Sur. Dannitt Abney. Wit. William Wright and John Cox. p 1

30 August 1788. Absalom BOSTICK and Mary Petty. Sur. T. M. Petty. p 12

3 January 1788. Obadiah BOSTICK and Nancy Colquitt. Sur. Jesse Spradling. Wit. Reubin Ragland, Jr. Nancy signs her own consent.
Married by Rev. John Atkinson. p 13

20 January 1798. Richard BOSTICK and Ann Link. Sur. William Link.
p 40

29 October 1785. Frederick BOTT and Elizabeth Comer, dau. Thomas Comer.
Sur. Moore Comer. See Frederick Boott. p 7

9 January 1790. Frederick BOTT and Sally Torian. Sur. William Thompson.
p 19

5 April 1786. Joel BOTT and Lucy May. Sur. George Carrington. Wit.
Agnes Cocke and Samuel Annat (?). Lucy May and Agnes May consent for
Lucy; no relationship stated. p 9

23 April 1800. Thomas BOTTOM and Betsey Robertson, dau. of Henry
Robertson who consents and is surety. Wit. Ennis Organ. p 44

24 November 1791. Alexander BOWMAN and Caty Newbill. Married by Rev.
Thomas Dobson. See Alexander Bomar. Ministers' Returns p 86

4 June 1788. Edward BOWMAN and Mary Wood. Married by Rev. Hawkins
Landrum. Ministers' Returns p 42

29 December 1788. Fielding BOWMAN and Caty Bowman, dau. William Bowman
who consents. Sur. Billy Bowman. Wit. Alexander Bowman. p 14

23 September 1795. John BOWMAN and Nancy Neely. Married by Rev.
Hawkins Landrum. See John Bowmar. Ministers' Returns p 111

15 May 1782. Thomas BOWMAN and Anne Thompson. Married by Rev.
Nathaniel Hall. Ministers' Returns p 206

29 October 1791. Alexander BOMAR and Catey Newbill. Sur. George
Newbill. See Alexander Bowman. p 22

8 September 1795. John BOWMAR and Nancy Neeley. Sur. William Neeley.
Wit. Edmond Chisom. Nancy signs her own consent. See John Bowman.
p 32

23 October 1797. Thomas BOWMAR and Elizabeth High. Sur. Benjamin High.
Married by Rev. Thomas Dobson. p 36

22 November 1769. Benjamin BOXLEY and Tabitha Irby. Sur. George Boyd.
Wit. Thomas Tunstall. p 2

7 May 1799. Harrison BOXLEY and Nancy Haynes, dau. Anna Haynes who
consents. Sur. Moore Comer. Wit. William Boxley. p 42

25 March 1799. Joseph BOXLEY and Susannah Boyd, dau. David Boyd who consents. Sur. Roy Boyd. Married 28 March by Rev. Reuben Pickett. p 42

18 July 1799. William BOXLEY and Elizabeth Bennett. Married by Rev. Rebuen Pickett. Ministers' Returns p 137

28 May 1792. Aaron BOYD and Betsy Younger, dau. William Younger who consents. Sur. David Brandon. p 26

26 January 1795. Abner BOYD and Polley Palmer. Sur. Edward Palmer. Married 29 January by Rev. Reuben Pickett. p 32

21 October 1776. David BOYD and Elizabeth Wiley. Sur. William Wiley. Wit. Henry Goare. p 3

1 January 1796. Edward BOYD and Isabella Camp. Sur. Richard Camp. Wit. Nancy Williams. George Camp, Sr. consents for Isabella; no relationship stated. Married 3 January by Rev. Alexander Hay. p 35

8 August 1786. Frances BOYD and Eliza Combes Estes. Sur. Moses Estes. Married 10 August by Rev. Hawkins Landrum who says <u>Clarisa</u> <u>Combs</u> Estes. p 10

6 January 1760. George BOYD, Jr. and Wilmoth Irby. Sur. Peter Irby. Wit. John Hamilton and Richard Finch. p 1

1 November 1797. George BOYD, Jr. and Leah Boyd. Sur. John Boyd. Wit. Robert Boyd. Consent of George Boyd, Sr., guardian of Leah, for her. Married by Rev. Leonard Baker. p 36

14 August 1786. Henry BOYD and Reform Winders, dau. Adam and Elizabeth Winders who consent. Sur. Andrew Douglass. p 8

6 January 1789. James BOYD and Sarah Gunter. Sur. William Epps. Writes her own consent signed <u>Sally</u> Gunter. Wit. William Gorley. Married 9 January by Rev. James Watkins. Bond on p 17 Ministers' Returns on p 33 and consent on p 12.

16 August 1789. James BOYD, Jr. and Polley Gunter, dau. Sarah Boyd who consents. Sur. Joshua Powell. Wit. William Watlington and James Powers. James married his step-mother's daughter by a former marriage. Married by Rev. Reuben Pickett, 21 August. p 17

4 January 1799. James BOYD and Ruthey Farmer, dau. Archer Farmer who consents. Sur. Jesse Boyd. Wit. Anderson J. Hurst. p 42

8 January 1790. Jesse BOYD and Lucy Griffin, dau. Anthony Griffin who consents and is surety. Wit. William Griffin. Married 19 January by Rev. William Moore. p 19

10 February 1789. John BOYD and Polly Crowder. Sur. James Boyd. Polly signs her own consent. Married 10 March by Rev. James Watkins. p 16

25 November 1793. John BOYD and Winifred Salmon. Sur. John Salmon. Married 10 December by Rev. James Watkins. p 28

7 May 1798. Lawson BOYD and Tabitha Holt, dau. Mary Holt who consents. Sur. John Holt. I think she was the daughter of Peter Holt, deceased. Married by Rev. Hawkins Landrum. p 40

22 December 1796. Lemuel BOYD and Drusilla Hardridge. Sur. Aaron Boyd. Drusilla signs her own consent. p 34

25 November 1785. Patrick BOYD and Sarah Adams. Sur. George Boyd. Wit. William P. Martin. John Adams consents for Sarah; no relationship stated. Married by Rev. Reubin Pickett. p 7

20 December 1791. Patrick BOYD and Jane Wade, dau. Charles Wade who consents. Sur. Moses Dunkley. Wit. B. W. Wade. p 21

29 February 1792. William Patrick BOYD and Margaret Estes, dau. Moses Estes who consents. Sur. Edward R. Watlington. Married 12 March by Rev. Alexander Hay. p 24

5 November 1792. William BOYD and Francina Cook. Sur. Benjamin Hall. Wit. George Parish. p 26

17 May 1798. William BOYD and Catey Juniel. Sur. Robert Juniel. Married by Rev. Leonard Baker. p 41

24 February 1800. William I. BOYD and Margaret Anderson. Sur. Robert Boyd. Wit. Joseph Pettey. Margaret signs her own consent. p 44

7 March 1795. John BRADSHAW and Ann Salmon. Married by Rev. James Watkins. Ministers' Returns p 106

17 January 1795. William BRADSHAW and Susanna Salmon, dau. John Salmon, Sr. who consents. Sur. Robert Salmon. Wit. Henry Salmon. Married 22 January by Rev. James Watkins. p 31

21 December 1790. Thomas BRADY and Frances Murphy. Sur. Francis Young. Wit. John Patterson. Signs her own consent as Fanny Murphy. Married by Rev. Hawkins Landrum. p 19

22 February 1790. Hugh BRAGG and Mary Miller. Sur. Joseph Hicks. Mary signs her own consent. Married 25 February by Rev. James Watkins. p 20

22 May 1792. Samuel D. BRAME and Elizabeth Goodwin, dau. Peter Goodwin who consents. Sur. Beal Goodwin. p 26

17 May 1785. David BRANDON and Catherine Irvine. Sur. John Irvine. Wit. Henry Goare. p 6

19 February 1782. Thomas BRANDON and Margaret Irvine. Sur. Abge (Abegail?) Irvine. Wit. Henry Goare. p 5

25 May 1789. Thomas BRANDON and Agatha Warrin, dau. James Warrin who consents. Sur. James Watkins. Wit. William Watkins. Married 28 May by Rev. James Watkins who says Agnes Warren. p 16

3 November 1797. Thomas BRANDON and Betsey Lawson. Sur. William Taylor. Married 9 November by Rev. James Watkins. p 36

7 March 1794. John BRATCHER and Anny Solomon. Sur. John Solomon. p 29

19 September 1785. James BRAY and Rebecca Bailey, dau. Joseph Bailey. Sur. Aaron Moseley. Married 22 September by Rev. Thomas Dobson. p 7

BREWER see BREWIS

13 February 1782. James BREWIS and Tabitha Musain. Married by Rev. Nathaniel Hall. This name may be Brewer. Ministers' Returns p 10

23 June 1794. Flemming BRIDGMAN and Polley Singleton, dau. James Singleton who consents. Sur. William Bays. Married by Rev. Hawkins Landrum. Returned 14 August. He says Fleming. p 29

24 April 1797. William BRITTON and Betsey Thweatt. Sur. Giles Thweatt. Married 11 May by Rev. Thomas Dobson. p 36

14 September 1800. John BROGAN and Elizabeth Owen, dau. Feby Owen (mother) who consents. Sur. Bracket Owen. p 44

9 February 1795. Bilbe (or Billie) BROOKS and Isbell Ashworth, dau. Samuel Ashworth who consents. Both of age. Sur. Joel Ashworth. Wit. William Brizentine and William Burchet. p 32

7 January 1783. David BROOKS and Ona Gravett. Sur. John Carmichail. Wit. Henry Goare. William Hobson consents for Ona; no relationship stated. p 6

3 January 1795. John BROOKS and Sarah Faulkner. Sur. Joseph Faulkner. Wit. Susanna Faulkner. Sarah signs her own consent. Married 8 January by Rev. Reuben Pickett. p 33

28 November 1789. Richard BROOKS and Nancy Nap Vaughan. Sur. Thomas Nap Vaughan. Married by Rev. James Watkins. p 17

28 March 1786. Robert BROOKS and Fanny Brooks, dau. John Brooks. Sur. John Ball. Wit. Joseph Hicks and James Watkins. p 8

19 January 1786. Thomas BROUGH and Margaret Roberson. Sur. Ann Rose Roberson. Married 22 January by Rev. Thomas Dobson who says Robinson. p 9

22 December 1795. Fleming BROWN and Elizabeth Whitehead. Sur. Lerick (?) Brown. Wit. Benjamin Dickson, Sr. and Lazarus Brown. Both Fleming and Elizabeth sign their own consents. Married 24 December by Rev. Hawkins Landrum. p 32

1 February 1790. James BROWN and Ruth Smallman, dau. John Smallman who consents. Sur. Elias Palmer. Married 4 February by Rev. James Watkins. p 19

5 August 1788. John BROWN and Mary Gholson. Sur. Frederick Brown. Married 9 August by Rev. James Watkins. p 12

22 December 1794. Langston BROWN and Sarah Evans. Sur. Robert Evans. Married by Rev. John Atkinson. p 29

6 December 1788. Martin BROWN and Caty Younger, dau. Thomas Younger who consents. Sur. Joseph Younger. Wit. Samuel Younger and John Winn. p 12

10 July 1794. Thomas BROWN and Mary Ashlock. Sur. Adam Foot. Married by Rev. Hawkins Landrum. p 29

24 March 1800. Watkins BROWN and Mourning Brown. Sur. John Brown. p 44

31 July 1799. James BRUCE and Sarah Coles. Sur. Charles Bruce. Married 1 August by Rev. Alexander Hay. p 42

17 January 1780. John BRUCE and Nancy Hoskins, dau. William Hoskins. Sur. Robert Wooding. Wit. William Hoskins, Jr., and Rebecca Watkins. p 4

23 June 1788. John BRUCE and Sarah Roberts. Sur. Francis Roberts. p 12

5 August 1793. Michail BRUCE and Mary Poor. Sur. Joseph Scats. Mary signs her own consent. Married 9 August by Rev. Thomas Dobson. p 27

10 November 1784. Joseph BRUNFIELD and Anne Street. Married by Rev. Nathaniel Hall. Ministers' Returns p 204

27 February 1786. Jesse BRUNWOOD and Fanny Sans. Sur. John Adams.
Consent of John Sans for Fanny; no relationship stated. See Jesse
Burnwood. p 10

8 November 1794. John BRYAN and Kitty Farguson, dau. Thomas Farguson
who consents. Wit. Stith Harrison and Elizabeth Farguson. Sur. Stith
Harrison. See John Bryant. p 29

13 November 1794. John BRYANT and Milley Farguson. Married by Rev.
Hawkins Landrum. See John Bryan. Ministers' Returns p 94

14 December 1785. Richard BUCK and Kindness Breedlove. Sur. James
Chappell. Wit. Mary Hunt and Sarah Waid (Wade). p 7

25 August 1788. James BUCKLEY and Mary Ridgeway. Sur. James Ridgeway.
p 14

27 April 1789. Randolph BUCKLEY and Mildred Oliver. Sur. Peter Thaxton.
Wit. E. Winders, John Chambers and William Stovall. Nicherson
Oliver consents for Mildred; no relationship stated. Married by Rev.
James Watkins. Returned 23 May. p 17

18 January 1786. Robert BURCKETT and Martha Sikes, dau. Elizabeth Sikes
who consents. Sur. James Sikes. Wit. Martha Sikes. Married by
Rev. Reubin Pickett. Return dated 18 February. p 9

8 April 1794. Henry BURGE and Mary White, dau. Tabitha White who
consents. Sur. William Burge. Married 10 April by Rev. Leonard
Baker. p 29

25 October 1790. Mordecai BURGESS and Mary Brandon, dau. Ellener
Brandon who consents. p 18

18 November 1795. William BURNES (BYRN) and Nancy Chandler. Sur.
William Chandler. Wit. Jonah Chandler. Nancy signs her own consent.
This bond is signed William Byrn and a note in the register says
Byrn is correct. Married 19 November by Rev. Hawkins Landrum. p 32

1 March 1786. Jesse BURNWOOD and Fanny Sans (Sands). Married by Rev.
Reubin Rickett. See Jesse Brunwood. Ministers' Returns p 13

3 September 1784. George BURRUS and June Leats. Married by Rev.
Nathaniel Hall. Ministers' Returns p 204

25 May 1795. James BURTON and Elizabeth Jones. Sur. Stephen Hughes.
Elizabeth signs her own consent. p 31

15 September 1787. John BUTLER and Nancy Cannaday, dau. William
Cannaday who consents. Sur. Neil Cannaday. Wit. John Singleton. p 11

16 June 1800. John BUTLER and Suckey Hughes, dau. John Hughes. Sur. Joseph Hughes. Married 19 June by Rev. Reuben Pickett. p 44

14 March 1796. Richard BUTLER and Sally Enroughty. Sur. Robert Throck-morton. Sally signs her own consent. Sally Darby in Ministers' Returns. Married by Rev. Samuel D. Brame. p 34

BYRN see BURNES

25 November 1799. John BYRNE, Jr. and Sarah Bryant. Sur. William Phelps. Wit. James McCraw. Sarah signs her own consent. Married 28 November by Rev. Hawkins Landrum. p 42

4 March 1782. Howard CAIN and Elizabeth Morefield. Sur. John Morefield. Wit. Henry Goare. p 5

7 December 1789. William CALDWELL and Betsy Stanfield. Sur. Thomas Stanfield. p 16

18 June 1792. Henry CARDWELL and Polly Hankla. Sur. Thomas Hankla. Polly signs her own consent. Married 21 June by Rev. Thomas Dobson who says Hankley. p 25

22 December 1795. Thomas CARDWELL and Mary Palmer, dau. Jeffery Palmer who consents. Sur. Moses Palmer. p 33

12 December 1791. William CARDWELL and Elizabeth Hankla. Sur. Thomas Hankla. Married 15 December by Rev. Thomas Dobson who says Hankley. p 20

3 September 1798. John CARMICAL and Elizabeth Childress. Sur. James Watkins. Wit. David Hix. Consent of Peter and Susanna Crews for Elizabeth Childress; no relationship stated. Peter Crews m. Susanna Childress 24 June 1797. Married 4 September by Rev. James Watkins. p 40

8 April 1799. Archibald CARNALL and Polly Lipscomb, dau. Thomas Lips-comb who consents. Sur. John Lipscomb. Married 11 April by Rev. Nathaniel Hollaway. p 42

23 December 1795. John CARR and Jane Priddy, dau. George Priddy who consents. Sur. William Carr. Wit. Dudley Glass, Jr. and James Priddy. p 33

16 April 1789. John CARRELL and Isbell Bowmar, dau. Thomas Bomar who consents. Sur. Fielding Bomar. Wit. John Bomar. Married 20 April by Rev. William Moore who says Bowman. p 17

1 April 1784. George CARRINGTON and Sarah Tucker. Sur. Isaac Coles. Wit. Joseph Haynes. p 6

24 August 1786. Paul CARRINGTON, Jr. and Mildred N. Coles. Sur. Isaac Coles. Wit. George Carrington and Mary Tucker. p 10

27 February 1792. Paul CARRINGTON and Priscilla Sims, dau. Daniel Sims who consents. Sur. William Thompson. Married 6 March by Rev. Hawkins Landrum. p 25

25 July 1793. Charles W. CARTER and Ursula Palmer. Married by Rev. Reuben Pickett. Ministers' Returns p 91

24 November 1783. Daniel CARTER and Sarah Richardson. Sur. Martin Barker. Wit. James Richardson, Margaret Richardson and Patty Dickie. Consent of Richard and Sarah Edwards guardians of Sarah. p 6

24 March 1794. George CARTER and Elizabeth Smith. Sur. Robin Cole. Elizabeth signs her own consent. p 29

4 April 1794. George CARTER and Elizabeth Cole. This is in the Ministers' Returns but not signed by a minister. Instead it is marked "Teste: George Carrington, Clerk." Ministers' Returns p 100

17 September 1792. Hartwell CARTER and Sally Colquett. Sur. John Terry Colquett. Sally signs her own consent. Married 20 September by Rev. Alexander Hay. p 26

25 January 1790. John CARTER and Sarah Farmer, dau. Frederick Farmer who consents. Sur. Enoch Farmer. Wit. Nipper Adams and George Newbill. p 18

14 September 1799. John CARTER and Sarah Blankenship. Sur. Jordan Clay. Consent of John Blankenship for Sarah; no relationship stated. p 42

17 June 1800. John CARTER and Sally Watkins. Sur. Robert Terry. Wit. Nancy Terry and Elizabeth Reade. Sally signs her own consent. Married 19 June by Rev. Alexander Hay. p 45

21 December 1786. Jonah CARTER and Sarah Morehead. Sur. Singleton Holt. Wit. William Peter Martin. p 8

4 April 1792. Joseph M. CARTER and Sally Faulkner. Married by Rev. Reuben Pickett. Ministers' Returns p 58

24 December 1790. Mathew CARTER and Elizabeth Nash. Married by Rev. Reuben Pickett. See Matthia Carter. Ministers' Returns p 62

10 December 1790. Matthias CARTER and Betsy Nash. Sur. William Epps. Betsy signs her own consent. See Mathew Carter. p 19

29 January 1789. Presley CARTER and Ann Waddle. Married by Rev. James
Watkins. Ministers' Returns p 38

26 October 1792. Robert CARTER and Unity Cook, dau. John Cook who
consents. Sur. William Yancy. Married 1 November by Rev. William
P. Martin. p 25

26 February 1798. Thomas CARTER and Mary Powell, dau. David Powell who
consents and is surety. Wit. James Bigger and Polly Carter.
Married 9 March by Rev. James Watkins. p 40

17 November 1800. Daniel CASSADY and Grace Mullins. Sur. James Mullins.
Married 18 November by Rev. Thomas Dobson who says Jenny Mullins. p 45

20 October 1786. Josiah Walker CATHIEL and Betty Legrand. Sur. John
Morehead. Both Josiah and Betty sign their own consents. p 8

26 December 1786. Josiah CATEHALE and Sarah Morehead. Married by Rev.
Thomas Dobson. Ministers' Returns p 25

27 August 1798. Ludy CAUTHRON and Mary Bush. Sur. Thomas Bush.
Married 1 September by Rev. Hawkins Landrum. p 40

13 November 1797. James CHALMERS and Sarah Watkins. Sur. Philip Vass.
Sarah signs her own consent. p 35

2 May 1780. Robert Erskine CHAMBERS and Milliscent Dennis. Sur. Black-
mon Ligon. Wit. Henry Goare. Robert Jones signs the certificate.
p 4

26 December 1796. Thomas CHAMBERS and Polly Pryor. Sur. William Murray.
Polly signs her own consent. Married 5 January 1797 by Rev. Nathaniel
Holloway who says Paynor. p 35

25 November 1788. William CHAMBERS and Nancy Oliver. Consent of Richard
Oliver for Nancy; no relationship stated. Sur. Thomas Turner.
Married 4 December by Rev. James Watkins. p 13

27 March 1792. William CHAMBERS and Agnes Oliver. Sur. Randolph
Buckley. Consent of N. Oliver for Agnes; no relationship stated.
Married by Rev. Nathaniel Holloway. p 25

17 January 1796. Frederick CHANDLER and Isbell Seemster? Sur. Elias
Palmer. Consent of John Seemster for Isabell; no relationship stated.
p 35

10 January 1775. John CHANDLER and Caty Tunstall. Sur. Thomas Tunstall.
Wit. Mary Chandler. John son of Robert Chandler. p 3

18 October 1792. Josiah CHANDLER and Polly Roberts. Married by Rev. Thomas Dobson. Ministers' Returns p 82

6 July 1791. William CHANDLER and Polly Hill, dau. William Hill. Sur. John Yeates. Married 7 July by Rev. Thomas Dobson who says Mary. p 21

30 June 1792. William CHANDLER and Betsy Roberts. Sur. Josiah Chandler. Married 5 July by Rev. Thomas Dobson. p 26

12 January 1787. Abram CHANEY and Mary Cheatham, dau. Robert Cheatham who consents. Sur. Thomas Fornby. See Abraham China. p 11

12 January 1788. Nathan CHANEY and Elizabeth Cheatham, dau. Robert Cheatham who consents. Sur. John Chaney. Married by Rev. John Atkinson. p 13

24 January 1791. John CHAPMAN and Lucy Williams, dau. Luke Williams who consents. Sur. Charles Irby. p 20

23 December 1789. Moses CHAPMAN and Sally Tuck. Sur. Cary Tuck. Sally signs her own consent. Married 25 December by Rev. Hawkins Landrum. p 16

30 April 1796. William CHAPMAN and Lucy Tuck. Sur. Cary Tuck. Lucy signs her own consent. Married 9 May by Rev. Thomas Dobson. p 34

22 January 1781. James CHAPPELL and Martha Wooding, dau. Robert Wooding who consents. Wit. Thomas Hill and Richard Long. Sur. William Terry. Wit. Henry Goare. This may be June. She is mentioned in her father's will 1797. p 5

12 January 1790. James CHAPPELL and Lucy Woodson, dau. John Woodson who consents. Sur. Thomas Davenport. Married 14 January by Rev. James Watkins. p 19

5 December 1799. Joel CHAPPELL and Tabitha Light. Married by Rev. Hawkins Landrum. Ministers' Returns p 145

15 March 1781. John CHAPPELL and Sarah Dickie, dau. John Dickie. Sur. Moses Johnson. Wit. Henry Goare. p 5

27 April 1789. John CHAPPELL and Nancy DeGraffenread. Sur. William Hamlett. Wit. John Dickie. Nancy signs her own consent. p 16

7 February 1793. Leonard CHEATHAM and Letty Edwards. Sur. Edward W. Wade. Letty signs her own consent. Married by Rev. Thomas Dobson. p 28

18 December 1793. George CHELTON and Luvany Combs. Sur. Jesse Foster. Wit. Joseph Dobson. Luvany signs her own consent. See George Shelton. p 28

27 May 1793. Mark CHELTON and Nancy Dodson. Sur. Fortunatus Dodson. Wit. Joseph Dodson. Nancy signs her own consent. See Mark Shelton. p 28

23 December 1790. William CHEANAULT and Margaret Mann. Sur. Nelson Abraham. Wit. John Chenault. Margaret signs her own consent. Married by Rev. Jesse Owen. p 18

28 July 1796. William CHESSER and Anne League. Sur. Vincent Wyatt. Anne signs her own consent. p 34

December 1789. Harden CHICK and Nancy Scates, dau. Margrie Granell who consents. Sur. William Chick. Wit. James Granells and Mary Scates. p 16

30 December 1785. Richard CHILDRES and Jane Weaver. Married by Rev. Thomas Dobson. See Richard Childrey. Ministers' Returns p 15

26 May 1788. Robert CHILDRESS and Jane Gresham. Sur. Anthony Gresham. Jane signs her own consent. p 13

10 July 1796. Robert CHILDRESS and Becky Bradley, dau. James Bradley who consents. Sur. Jesse Bradley. p 34

30 December 1785. Richard CHILDREY and Jane Weaver. Sur. John Weaver. Wit. Frederick Vaughan. Jane signs her own consent. See Richard Childres. p 7

13 October 1797. Benjamin F. CHILES and Betsy Faulkner, dau. Johnson Faulkner who consents. Sur. Jacob Faulkner. Wit. William Faulkner. Married 17 October by Rev. Reuben Pickett. p 35

15 January 1787. Abraham CHINA and Mary Cheatham. Married by Rev. John Atkinson. See Abram Chaney. Ministers' Returns p 26

20 October 1785. Edmund CHISUM and Polly Chandler. Sur. James Chisum. Wit. William P. Martin. Married by Rev. William Dodson. Returned in December. p 7

6 July 1796. James CHISUM and Johanna Phelps. Sur. Edmund Chisum. Johanna signs her own consent. Married 7 July by Rev. Hawkins Landrum who says Joanah. p 34

21 December 1778. William CHRISTOPHER and Lucy Jones, dau. Richard Jones. Sur. Thomas Erskine. Wit. Richard Jones, Jr. p 3

23 August 1790. David CHUMLEY and Mary Mays. Sur. James Smith. Married 31 August by Rev. William Moore. p 17

11 February 1793. John CHUMLEY and Elizabeth Mase. Sur. Obad Hendrick. Wit. Beverly Mase. Elizabeth signs her own consent. This name may be Muse. p 27

14 June 1800. John CHUMLEY and Isabell Boyd. Sur. David Boyd. p 44

- -   1793. Robert CHURCH and Mary Pickett. Married by Rev. John Atkinson. Ministers' Returns p 91

11 February 1795. Michael CLARDY and Nancy Comer. Sur. John London. Wit. Charles Jenkins. Nancy signs her own consent. p 33

26 October 1789. Thomas CLARDY and Mary Henderson. Sur. Daniel Henderson. Mary signs her own consent. Married by Rev. William Moore. p 16

- -   1786. John CLARK and Susanna Royall. Sur. David Clark. p 10

21 September 1790. John CLARK and Nancy Bray. Sur. Heyman Dyer. p 17

25 March 1793. David CLARKE and Betsey Sims. Sur. John Clark. Consent of Little Joe Morton, guardian of Elizabeth Sims. Married 28 March by Rev. Thomas Dobson. p 28

5 June 1797. Thomas CLARKE and Mary T. Hill. Sur. John Hill. Wit. Coleman Williams. Mary signs her own consent. p 36

13 May 1796. Jordan CLAY and Mary Carter. Sur. John Carter. Wit. James Whalen and Huriah Francis. p 34

30 January 1792. Josiah CLAY and Elizabeth Claiborn West, dau. Abraham West who consents. Sur. William Piles. Married 2 February by Rev. Jesse Owen. p 25

29 March 1771. Maston CLAY and Elizabeth Williams, dau. John Williams. Sur. Samuel Burks. p 2

29 July 1782. Samuel CLAY and Patty Wall. Sur. David Wall. Wit. Henry Goare. p 5

22 December 1788. William C. CLAY and Rebeckah Comer. Sur. Bedford Davenport. p 13

15 June 1793. John CLAYBROOK and Susannah McFarlin. Sur. John Terrell. Wit. William Wade and James Terrell. Susannah signs her own consent. p 28

12 November 1798. Stephen CLEMENT and Susanna Palmer. Sur. Jeffrey Palmer. Married by Rev. Thomas Dobson. p 40

23 October 1797. Edmund CLOWDIS and Judy Medley, dau. Mehitabel Medley who consents. Sur. Francis Clowdes. Wit. David Vaughan. Married 26 October by Rev. James Watkins. p 37

14 April 1800. Francis CLOWDER and Lucy Goodwyn, dau. David Goodwyn who consents. Sur. Archelaus Goodwyn. Married 16 April by Rev. James Watkins. p 45

19 January 1793. James CLOWDIS and Elizabeth Wily. Sur. Edmund Clowdis. See James Crowders. p 27

9 June 1794. Richard COATES and Polley Coates. Sur. Benjamin Hunt. Wit. Rachel Coats. Polley signs her own consent. Married by Rev. Thomas Dobson. p 29

19 January 1797. Ambrose COBBS and Susanna Bradley, dau. James Bradley who consents. Sur. Jesse Bradley. p 37

20 December 1791. Henry COCKE and Patsy Wood, dau. Thomas Wood who consents. Sur. John Wood. See Henry Coxe. p 20

25 August 1798. Herbert C. COCKE and Salley Roberts. Sur. Edward Roberts. William Roberts, guardian of Salley consents for her. William Thompson, guardian of Herbert C. Cocke consents for him. Married 29 August by Rev. Alexander Hay. p 40

22 December 1796. Jacob COE and Jemima Terrell. Sur. Richard Terrell. p 34

9 August 1788. Esau COLE and Nancy Yates, dau. Francis Yates who consents. Sur. William Yates. Married by Rev. John Atkinson. p 12

28 December 1789. Robert COLE and Nancy Carter. Sur. Richard Carter. Married 31 December by Rev. Hawkins Landrum. p 16

10 December 1799. Daniel COLLINS and Ann Boyd. Married by Rev. Reuben Pickett. Ministers' Returns p 141

21 February 1783. Elisha COLLINS and Frances Madison. Married by Rev. Nathaniel Hall. Ministers' Returns p 204

26 August 1800. George COLLINS and Betsey Powell, dau. Thomas Powell who consents. Sur. Burges Harelson. Married 27 August by Rev. Reuben Pickett. p 45

28 September 1795. James COLLINS and Elizabeth Lovelace, dau. Tabitha Lovelace who consents. Sur. Nathaniel Lovelace. (Bond says Tabitha but consent, signed by Tabitha says "my dau. Elizabeth". Also see deed 25 June 1810 from James Collins and Elizabeth, his wife.) Married by Rev. Samuel D. Brame. p 33

5 November 1782. Jeremiah COLLINS and Mary Pulliam. Married by Rev. Nathaniel Hall. Ministers' Returns p 206

26 December 1782. Thomas COLLINS and Elizabeth Craddock. Married by Rev. Nathaniel Hall. Ministers' Returns p 9

28 April 1800. Thomas COLLINS and Sally McCarty. Sur. William Blane. Wit. John Isbell. Sally signs her own consent. Married 1 May by Rev. Reuben Pickett. p 45

28 January 1795. Achilles COLQUETT and Mary Franklin. Sur. J. H. Colquett. Wit. Henry Colquett. Mary signs her own consent. Married by Rev. Alexander Hay. p 33

4 January 1788. Frederick COLQUETT and Mary Stubblefield, dau. George and Keziah Stubblefield who consents. Sur. Jesse Spradling. Married by Rev. John Atkinson. p 13

12 September 1796. Henry COLQUETT and Nancy S. Holt. Sur. Singleton Holt. Wit. Peyton Holt. Simon Holt consents for Nancy; no relationship stated. Married 15 September by Rev. John Atkinson. p 35

24 February 1794. Permenas COLQUETT and Lucy Davenport. Sur. Tha. Davenport. Married 20 March by Rev. Alexander Hay who says Permemas. p 29

8 February 1786. Frederick COLQUITT and Elizabeth Bolt. Sur. Obediah Gent. Wit. Obediah Baughstock. Frederick son of Jonathan Colquitt. The name Baughstock also spelled Bostock and Bostick. p 9

20 July 1786. John T. COLQUITT and Alice (or Alcie) Dickie. Married by Rev. James Watkins. Ministers' Returns p 20

25 November 1785. Ransome COLQUIT and Susannah Baker. Sur. Obadiah Gent. Wit. Henrietta Baker. Susannah signs her own consent. Married by Rev. Hawkins Landrum. p 7

17 April 1786. Charles COMBO and Elizabeth Mashell. Sur. William Powell. Wit. William Peter Martin. Married by Rev. Hawkins Landrum. Returned 7 September. Probably Marshall. p 9

19 August 1794. John COMBOW (CUMBO) and Polley Jennings. Sur. Bolling Hamlett. Wit. William East. Polley signs her own consent. p 31

4 November 1786. Archibald COMER and Rachel Boyd. Sur. Peter Follis. Married 7 December by Rev. Reuben Pickett. p 9

1 April 1799. Moore COMER and Dorothy Ragland. Sur. Jesse Munday. p 42

17 December 1799. Thomas CONNALLY and Susanna Ball. Sur. Carter Ball. p 42

24 October 1792. William CONNELY and Nancy Tune. Sur. Robert Neely. Married by Rev. Jesse Owen. p 26

18 January 1787. William CONSTANT and Darcus Weaver. No surety given. Wit. Peter Wilson and Robert Wilson. Both sign their own consents. Married by Rev. Hawkins Landrum who says Dorcas. p 10

24 April 1797. Edmund COOK and Mary Dismuke, dau. Elisha Dismuke who consents. Sur. John Miller. Married by Rev. John Atkinson. Return dated 24 June. p 35

19 January 1800. Jarratt W. COOK and Elizabeth Carter, dau. Frances Carter who consents. Sur. Spencer Carter. Wit. Franey Carter. Married by Rev. John Atkinson who says Jarrad. p 45

27 November 1797. Henry COVENTON and Polly Blackstone. Sur. William Blackstone. Married 30 November by Rev. Thomas Dobson who says Covington. p 35

COVINGTON see COVENTON

27 September 1788. John COVINGTON and Susanna Walker Tomson. Sur. Thomas Puckett. Wit. Dicey Covington and Elizabeth Puckett. p 13

8 February 1783. James COX and Jurian Hardwick. Married by Rev. Nathaniel Hall. Ministers' Returns p 8

1 November 1766. John COX and Mary Farguson. Sur. John Orvil Turnstall. Wit. James Drummond. p 2

22 March 1790. Samuel COX and Katty Bruce. Sur. John Bruce. Married 24 March by Rev. James Watkins who says Caty. p 17

22 December 1791. Henry COXE and Patsy Wood. Married by Rev. Hawkins Landrum. See Henry Cocke. Ministers' Returns p 56

17 February 1790. Edward CRABTREE and Patsy Puckett, dau. Anthony
Puckett who consents. Sur. David Puckett. Married by Rev. John
Atkinson. p 19

4 March 1797. James CRENSHAW and Patsey Shelton, dau. Elizabeth Shelton
who consents. Sur. Bartlett Crenshaw. p 36

18 July 1794. Lewis CRENSHAW and Sarah Douglass. Sur. William Douglass.
Wit. George Douglass. Sarah signs her own consent. Married 24 July
by Rev. Leonard Baker. p 29

22 December 1789. John CREWES and Ruth Hunt, dau. Ambrose Hunt who
consents. Sur. Larkin Cosley. Wit. Iago Deth and Jon Johns.
Married 24 December by Rev. James Watkins. p 16

28 November 1792. Andrew CREWS and Retter Bradley, dau. James Bradley
who consents. Sur. Peter Crews. Married 29 November by Rev. Jesse
Owen. p 25

29 December 1790. David CREWS and Drucilla Jones. Sur. Luke Lipscomb.
Wit. William Thompson. Consent of William Jones for Drucilla; no
relationship stated. p 19

2 January 1797. John CREWS and Elizabeth Samson, dau. Frances Samson
who consents. Sur. Jesse Samson. Married 12 January by Rev. Hawkins
Landrum. p 35

24 June 1797. Peter CREWS and Susannah Childress. Sur. Benjamin Lax.
Wit. William Lax. Susannah signs her own consent. p 35

24 November 1795. Richard CREWS and Susannah Jones. Sur. William
Jones. Wit. Andrew McGinis. p 33

14 February 1786. Charles CROSS and Prissey Tenney. Sur. Richard
Oliver. Prissey signs her own consent. Married by Rev. James Watkins.
p 9

31 July 1790. Featherstone CROSS and Elizabeth Runnals. Sur. William
Chapman. Elizabeth signs her own consent. Married 5 August by Rev.
Reuben Pickett who says Reynolds. p 19

24 January 1793. James CROWDERS and Elizabeth Wiley. Married by Rev.
James Watkins. See James Clowdis. Ministers' Returns p 78

9 February 1786. George CRYMES and Anne Dudley. Sur. William Hamlett,
Jr. p 9

1 December 1800. William CUCKSEE (COOKSEY?) and Mary Wyatt, dau. John
Wyatt who consents. Sur. Eliel Wyatt. Wit. William Compton. p 45

CUMBO see COMBO

28 December 1785. Peter CUMBO and Milly Ramsey. Sur. Charles Cumbo.
Wit. John Perkins and Thomas Cumbo. Milly signs her own consent.
Married 29 December by Rev. Hawkins Landrum. p 8

28 December 1795. John DAMERON and Elizabeth Boyd. Sur. John Boyd.
Wit. George Dameron. Sarah Dameron consents for Elizabeth. Married
31 December by Rev. Reuben Pickett. p 32

8 June 1783. George DAMMON and Sarah Boyd. This marriage is in the
Ministers' Returns but no name is signed. Ministers' Returns p 204

28 April 1800. Chesley DANIEL and Nancy Sims, dau. John Sims who consents. Sur. George Camp. Wit. John Morton and Martha Daniel.
Married 3 April by Rev. Thomas Dobson. p 45

3 January 1785. David DANIEL and Polly Warring Day, dau. Thomas Day.
Sur. Henry Colquitt. Wit. James Davenport and Joseph Holt. p 6

26 March 1789. George DANIEL and Margaret Wilson. Sur. Nimrod Farguson.
Married 27 March by Rev. William Moore. p 16

4 February 1780. James DANIEL and Drucilla Daniel. Sur. Robert Wooding.
Wit. Moses Johnson, Smith Johnson and Byrd Terry. Drucilla signs
her own consent. p 4

17 February 1790. Littleberry DANIEL and Keziah London. Sur. Poindexter
Daniel. Keziah signs her own consent. p 17

29 November 1785. Royal DANIEL and Nancy Willingham, dau. Jar'd Willingham. Sur. Tavner (?) Nance. Wit. David Daniel and Daniel Terry.
Married by Rev. Thomas Dobson who says Winningham. p 6

14 April 1792. Terry DANIEL and Frances Parker, dau. Richard Parker
who consents and is surety. Wit. Thomas Parker. Married 15 April
by Rev. Thomas Dobson. p 25

27 December 1790. Henry DAVENPORT and Anne Davenport. Sur. William
Douglass. Anne signs her own consent. Married 6 January 1791
by Rev. Alexander Hay. p 19

2 December 1796. James DAVENPORT and Jincey Hart, dau. Caleb and Mary
Hart who consent. Sur. Ellis Smith. p 34

21 March 1799. Thomas DAVENPORT and Jane Davenport. Sur. Permenas
Colquitt. Married 28 March by Rev. James Watkins. p 42

26 August 1792. William DAVENPORT and Sally Holt, dau. Molly Holt who consents. Sur. William Douglass. p 25

13 November 1790. Adam DAVIS and Winney Shelton, dau. Charles Shelton who consents. Sur. Jesse Davis. Married by Rev. John Atkinson. p 18

7 December 1792. Benjamin DAVIS and Polly Mullins. Sur. Jonathan Davis. Consent of Jesse Davis, guardian of Polly Mullins. Married 20 December by Rev. John Atkinson. p 25

30 November 1785. Jesse DAVIS, planter and Sarah Kirby. Sur. Joseph Kirby. Wit. William P. Martin. p 7

5 May 1772. William DAVIS and Susanna Wells (widow). Sur. Thomas Tunstall. Wit. Mary Tunstall. p 2

15 December 1797. John DEGRAFFENREID and Elizabeth King. Sur. John King. p 35

20 December 1789. Vincent DEGRAFFENREID and Martha Thaxton, dau. William Thaxton who consents. Sur. John Wealch. Wit. George Thaxton. Married 31 December by Rev. Reuben Pickett. p 17

26 December 1799. William DEGRAFFENRIED and Martha King. Married by Rev. Reuben Pickett. Ministers' Returns p 141

6 December 1794. Daniel DEJARNETT and Nancy Smith, dau. William Smith who consents. Sur. William Brumfield. p 29

7 September 1791. James DEJARNETT and Elizabeth Pillar. Sur. George Seamore. Wit. Daniel Dejarnett and George Dejarnett. Both James and Elizabeth sign their own consents. p 23

5 May 1772. John DENNIS and Millicent Jones. Sur. Richard Jones. Wit. Thomas Tunstall. p 3

10 October 1787. Archibald DICKERSON and Mary Organ. Sur. John Maxey. Mary signs her own consent. p 12

24 -   1784. John DICKIE and Alice Townes. Sur. Caleb Townes. Wit. Henry Goare. p 6

31 March 1788. John DICKIE and Patsey Vaughan. Sur. James Vaughan. Married 3 April by Rev. James Watkins. p 13

21 September 1780. Benjamin DICKSON and Elizabeth Whitehead (widow). Sur. Paul Carrington. Wit. Henry Goare. p 4

5 December 1792. Benjamin DICKSON and Elizabeth Farmer. Sur. Allen Whitehead. Elizabeth signs her own consent. Married 11 December by Rev. Jesse Owen who says Dixon. p 25

28 August 1797.   John DICKSON and Mary Dickson.   Sur. Thomas Dickson.
p 37

11 May 1778.   Stephen DICKSON and Nancy Edmunds.   Sur. Francis Edmunds.
Wit. Henry Goare.   p 3

20 December 1771.   Thomas DICKSON and Martha Adams, dau. Elener (Eleanor)
Adams.   Sur. Benjamin Dickson.   Wit. Joshua Adams.   p 2

27 October 1800.   Fielding DILLARD and Patsey Bradley.   Sur. William
Bradley.   p 45

22 December 1788.   Thomas DILLON and Nancy Bailey.   Sur. John Bailey.
p 13

24 September 1792.   Thomas DILLON and Sally Murphy.   Sur. William
Murphy.   Married 27 September by Rev. Thomas Dobson.   p 25

3 January 1798.   Daniel DISMUKES and Nancy Townes, dau. Caleb Townes who
consents.   Sur. Byrd Womack.   Wit. John Dismukes.   p 40

DIXON see DICKSON

15 September 1763.   Henry DIXON and Martha Wynn, dau. William Wynn who
is surety.   Wit. Thomas Tunstall.   p 1

22 August 1791.   Joseph DIXON and Susanna Hummins.   Sur. William Hamlett.
Susanna signs her own consent.   p 20

22 September 1788.   Elias DOBSON and Sally Stovall.   Sur. Jesse Stovall.
p 14

19 April 1793.   Thomas DOBSON and Polly Coleman.   Sur. John Penticost.
Wit. Joseph Ligon.   Polly signs her own consent.   Married 20 April
by Rev. Thomas Dobson who says Thomas E. Dobson.   p 28

23 November 1785.   Elias DODSON and Nancy Stamps.   Sur. Thomas Dodson.
Certificate signed by John Stamps; no relationship stated.   Nancy
signs her own consent.   p 6

2 December 1789.   Elijah DODSON and Sally Dodson, dau. William Dotson
who consents.   Sur. Henry Barnes.   p 17

21 May 1789.   Elisha DODSON and Hannah Lawson.   Sur. Hohn Russell.
Married by Rev. John Atkinson.   p 15

23 September 1793.   Fortunatus DODSON and Frances Hanks.   Sur. William
Dodson.   Frances signs her own consent.   p 28

19 March 1793. Jesse DODSON and Judith COMBS. Sur. Mark Chelton. Wit. Isaac Dodson and George Chelton. Signs her own consent as <u>Judah</u> Combs. Married by Rev. John Atkinson who says Judith. p 28

22 October 1789. Presley DODSON and Elizabeth Bates. Sur. Fleming Bates. Elizabeth signs her own consent. Married by Rev. John Atkinson. p 16

27 August 1798. Thomas DODSON and Cloe Bates. Sur. Ransdell Petty. Wit. Joseph Dodson. Cloe signs her own consent. Married by Rev. John Atkinson. p 41

10 May 1793. John DOUGLAS and Mary Brawner, dau. Benjamin Brawner who consents. Sur. Thomas Douglas. p 28

18 December 1798. John DOUGLAS and Hannah Douglas. Sur. Harrison Atkins. Wit. Edward Akin and Robert Jones. Hannah signs her own consent. p 40

15 November 1790. Andrew DOUGLASS and Susanna Willis. Sur. Epenetus Winders. Wit. John P. Chambers, George Douglass, and Henry Boyd. Consent of Robert Willis and Susanna Willis; no relationship stated. Married 18 November by Rev. Reuben Pickett. p 19

12 October 1791. George DOUGLASS and Elizabeth McFarland. Sur. William Douglas. Consent of Susanna McFarland for Elizabeth; no relationship stated. Married by Rev. Alexander Hay. p 20

24 August 1789. James DOUGLASS and Judith Wall, dau. Ursley Wall who consents. Sur. Thomas Douglass. Dau. of John Wall who m. Ursula Bates 19 January 1763; dau. of John Bates. Married by Rev. John Atkinson. p 15

30 April 1796. Nathaniel DOUGLASS and Polly Douglass. Sur. John Jones. Married by Rev. William Moore. p 34

22 November 1790. Thomas DOUGLASS and Betsy Davenport. Sur. Bedford Davenport. Married 1 December by Rev. William P. Martin. p 19

20 January 1791. William DOUGLASS and Betsy Holt. Married by Rev. Alexander Hay. Ministers' Returns p 63

12 April 1791. William DOUGLASS and Anne Crenshaw. Sur. Bartlet Estes. Anne signs her own consent. Married 14 April by Rev. Hawkins Landrum. p 23

20 January 1791. William DOUGLASS and Betsy Holt. Married by Rev. Alexander Hay. p 20

18 October 1797. James DRINKARD and Dicey Owen, dau. Feley Owen (mother)
who consents. Sur. Brackett Owen. Wit. John Martin and Moza Adams.
p 37

1 August 1766. James DRUMMOND and Ann Farguson. Sur. John Orvil
Tunstall. Wit. Thomas Tunstall. p 1

10 January 1800. William DRUMMOND and Sally Perkins. Sur. Tommy
Maskill. Sally signs her own consent. Married 11 January by Rev.
Hawkins Landrum. p 44

6 August 1755. Richard DUDGEON and Mary Terry. Sur. James Terry who
consents for Mary. Wit. Jeremiah Terry, John Dudgeon and William
Wright. p 1

11 November 1794. Henry DUNKLEY and Susanna Megrigs. Sur. John Dunkley.
Wit. Nancy Dunkley. Susanna signs her own consent. p 29

25 April 1797. John DUNKLEY and Tabitha Monday. Sur. Jesse Monday.
Tabitha signs her own consent. p 37

24 July 1784. Moses DUNKLEY and Sarah Prindel, dau. David Prindel.
Sur. Henry Goare. Wit. William Epps, John Dunkley and Peach Prindle.
p 6

15 October 1799. Absalom DUNN and Nancy Jinkins, dau. Robert Jinkins who
consents. Sur. Gentry Jinkins. Wit. H. F. Clark. Married 17
October by Rev. Thomas Dobson. p 42

18 July 1794. John DUNN, Jr. and Nancy Smith, dau. Sarah Smith who
consents. Sur. William Chandler. Wit. William Jennings and John
Follis. Married by Rev. Samuel D. Brame. p 29

22 March 1790. Joseph DUNN and Susannah Parker. Sur. Edmund Wade.
Signs her own consent as Suzanna Parker. p 18

19 April 1790. Daniel DURHAM and Polly Faulkner. Sur. James Palmer.
Wit. Charles Hood. Polly signs her own consent. Married 22 April
by Rev. Reuben Pickett. p 19

27 November 1797. John DURHAM and Martha Mullins. Sur. James Mullins.
Married 28 November by Rev. Thomas Dobson. p 37

2 July 1792. Thomas DYER and Polly Rogers. Sur. John May. Polly signs
her own consent. Married 5 July by Rev. Reuben Pickett. p 23

6 December 1790. Jubal EARLEY and Polly Cheatham, dau. Leonard Cheatham
who consents. Sur. Alexander Irvine. Married 9 December by Rev.
Alexander Hay. p 18

15 February 1787. Daniel EASLEY and Sarah Moore. Sur. David Franklin. p 11

23 November 1791. Daniel EASLEY and Edith Anderson. Sur. Isaac Easley. Married 24 November by Rev. Hawkins Landrum. p 23

11 December 1799. Drury EASLEY and Susannah Faulkner. Sur. Jacob Faulkner. Susannah signs her own consent. Married 26 December by Rev. Reuben Pickett. p 41

23 May 1791. Henry EASLEY and Anne Easley, dau. Worham Easley. Sur. Benjamin Word. Married 26 May by Rev. Hawkins Landrum. p 22

10 March 1778. Robert EASLEY and Wineyfred Dixon. Sur. Stephen Easley. Wit. Henry Goare. p 3

9 May 1798. Samuel EASLEY and Kitty Faulkner, dau. Frances Faulkner who consents. Sur. Edmund Hoskins. Wit. Horatio Wade and Elizabeth Fontaine. p 39

6 November 1789. Richard EAST and Drusilla Chapman, dau. John Chapman who consents. Sur. William East. Married by Rev. John Atkinson. p 15

26 September 1792. Edward EASTHAM and Christina Chany Chandler. Sur. Thomas Roberts. Christina signs her own consent. Married 28 September by Rev. Thomas Dobson. p 26

16 February 1769. James ECHOLS and Elizabeth Palmer (widow). Sur. William Todd. p 2

29 December 1787. Jeremiah ECHOLS and Elizabeth Dillon. Sur. Samuel Hubbard. p 12

17 February 1784. John ECHOLS and Franer Fornley. Sur. Nicholas Fornley. Wit. Henry Goare. p 6

13 January 1770. Obadiah ECHOLS and Catherine McDaniel, dau. William McDaniel. Sur. Thomas Tunstall. Wit. Luke Williams and James Echols. p 2

9 June 1791. Obediah ECHOLS and Lucy Atkinson. Married by Rev. Jesse Owen. Ministers' Returns p 60

10 December 1786. Alexander EDSON and Rhoda Dodson. Married by Rev. John Atkinson. Ministers' Returns p 26

30 April 1779. Charles EDWARDS and Lettuce Wade. Sur. Stephen Wade. Wit. Henry Goare. p 4

24 October 1791. John EDWARDS and Elizabeth Edwards, dau. Elizabeth
Edwards who consents. Sur. Richard Edwards. p 23

12 November 1800. Richard EDWARDS and Rhoda Tabor. Sur. Berryman Green.
Married 13 November by Rev. Reuben Pickett. p 45

22 February 1796. Stephen EDWARDS and Jenny Irvine. Sur. John Irvine.
p 34

25 December 1800. William EDWARDS and Sally Coleman. Sur. Benjamin
Word. Married by Rev. James Watkins. p 45

22 December 1785. Zachariah ELLETT and Assu West. Sur. Worham Easley.
Wit. Daniel Moore. Assu signs her own consent. Married 1 January
1786 by Rev. Thomas Dobson who says Eater West. p 7

10 September 1787. Richard EPPERSON and Polley Stewart, dau. John
Stewart who consents. Sur. Elias Washer. Wit. James Chapel. p 11

28 February 1792. William EPPES and Martha Dunkley. Sur. Moses Dunkley.
Wit. Henry Dunkley. Martha signs her own consent. Married
29 February by Rev. Thomas Dobson. p 23

6 December 1792. Ambrose ESTES and Milly Henson. Sur. James Brown.
Milly signs her own consent. Married by Rev. Thomas Dobson. p 24

16 December 1786. Bartlett ESTES and Rachel Pounds. Bartlett son of
Moses Estes who is surety. Wit. John Douglas. Married 19 December
by Rev. Hawkins Landrum. p 9

19 December 1786. George ESTES and Mary Younger, dau. Mark Younder who
consents. Sur. Daniel Parker. Married by Rev. Hawkins Landrum.
p 9

23 March 1795. Samuel ESTES and Sally Juniel, dau. Ann Juniel who
consents. Sur. Andrew Juniel. Wit. William Perry and Philip Roberts.
p 32

4 February 1792. William EVANS and Ruth Medcalf. Sur. Carson Guthrey.
William and Ruth both sign their own consents. Married 14 February
by Rev. James Watkins. p 23

19 August 1794. John FAGG and Elizabeth McCalester. Sur. William Flinn.
Wit. Thomas Ligon and Bonnet Gary. Elizabeth signs her own consent.
p 29

23 September 1793. Robert FAMBROUGH and Mary Gunston. Sur. Samuel
Weakley. Wit. John Organ. Mary signs her own consent. p 28

26 November 1796. Robert FAMBROUGH and Hannah Stewart. Sur. Robert Stewart. Hanna signs her own consent. p 35

6 November 1787. William FAMBROUGH and Phoebe Robertson, dau. Christopher Robertson who consents. Sur. William Gates. p 11

13 December 1786. Hudson FARGUSON and Rachel Hart. Sur. Thomas Vidito. Wit. John Farguson. Rachel signs her own consent. Married by Rev. John Atkinson who says Ferguson. p 10

7 January 1789. John FARGUSON and Sarah Anderson. Sur. John Anderson. Married 8 January by Rev. Hawkins Landrum who says Ferguson. p 16

10 December 1796. William FARGUSON and Salley Terrell, dau. James Terrell who consents. Sur. Benjamin Terrell. See William Ferguson. p 34

11 January 1799. Amos FARIS and Patsy Bass, dau. Henry Bass who consents. Wit. Peter Bass. This is consent only. p 41

23 July 1792. George FARLEY and Catherine Scott, dau. Rebeckah Scott who consents. Sur. William Scott. Wit. William Thompson. Married by Rev. Nathaniel Holloway. p 25

27 July 1789. Barnard FARMER and Molley Carr, dau. John Carr who consents. Sur. William Carr. p 17

3 October 1799. Benjamin FARMER and Jemimah Finch. Married by Rev. Hawkins Landrum. Ministers' Returns p 144

26 July 1790. Henry FARMER and Mary Sullins. Sur. Nathan Sullins. Married 3 August by Rev. William Moore. p 18

12 January 1790. Jeremiah FARMER and Easter Kerby, dau. Henry B. Kerby who consents. Sur. Jeremiah Kerby. Married 22 February by Rev. William Moore who says Esther. p 18

11 December 1787. Matthew FARMER and Molly Glass, dau. Dudley Glass who consents. Sur. Samuel White. Wit. John Glass and George Glass. p 10

19 December 1791. Abner FARRAR and Catherine Arrington. Sur. Allen Burton. Catherine signs her own consent. p 22

25 September 1797. Joshua FARRIS and Mary Compton, dau. Meredith Compton who consents. Sur. Amos Farris. Wit. James Buckley. p 37

5 August 1800. Benjamin FAULKNER and Susanna Blane, dau. Ephraim Blane who consents. Sur. James Howerton. Wit. Richard Fling. Married 28 August by Rev. Reuben Pickett. p 45

30 November 1786. John FAULKNER and Jane Jones. Married by Rev. Reuben Pickett. See Johnson Faulkner. p 19

20 November 1786. Johnson FAULKNER and Jane Jones. Sur. Stephen Hughes. Jane signs her own consent. See John Faulkner. p 9

28 October 1799. Joseph FAULKNER and Nancy Oakes, dau. Isaac Oakes who consents. Sur. Samuel Easley. Wit. Jacob Faulkner. Married 14 November by Rev. Alexander Hay. p 41

FERGUSON see FARGUSON

15 December 1796. William FERGUSON and Sally Ferrell. Married by Rev. William Moore. See William Farguson. Ministers' Returns p 117

- December 1798. Benjamin FERRELL and Elizabeth Hepson (Hobson?). Married by Rev. Nathaniel Holloway. Ministers' Returns p 128

16 August 1787. William FERRELL and Frances Martin. John Martin consents for Frances; no relationship stated. Sur. Nathan Sullins. Wit. William Walton. Married by Rev. John Atkinson. p 12

2 August 1800. Jesse FINCH and Caty Boyd. Sur. James Boyd. p 42

11 December 1792. William FINCH and Rebeckah Willingham. Sur. Jeremiah Willingham. Rebeckah signs her own consent. Married 12 December by Rev. Thomas Dobson. p 25

28 September 1795. John Henry FIRESHEETZ and Kesiah Jones. Sur. Job Jones. Signs her own consent as Kereal Jones. Married 29 September by Rev. William Moore. p 32

12 June 1797. William FINN and Margaret Martin. Sur. Jonathan Martin. Wit. Elizabeth Martin. Margaret signs her own consent. p 35

27 November 1798. Miles FINNEY and Fanny Haskins. Sur. Thomas Haskins. Married 1 December by Rev. Alexander Hay. p 39

6 May 1797. David FISHER and Creasia McKinney. Sur. William McKinney. Married 11 May by Rev. Thomas Dobson. p 37

22 April 1791. Henry FISHER and Constant Crews, dau. David Crews. Sur. John Fisher. p 23

24 May 1790. Thomas FISHER and Sarah Griffin. Sur. Anthony Griffin. Married by Rev. John Atkinson. p 18

16 May 1782. Walker FITTS and Susanna Pass, dau. Thomas Pass. Sur. John Pass. Wit. Henry Goare. p 5

18 July 1799. John W. FLEMING and Sally Roberts. Married by Rev. James Watkins. Ministers' Returns p 154

10 February 1790. Lewis FLEMISTER and Elly Chissum, dau. Barbary Chissum who consents. Sur. Edmund Chissum. Married 27 February by Rev. Hawkins Landrum. p 18

24 April 1787. William FLYNN and Sarah Wright. Sur. John Flynn. Wit. Hampton White and William Mullen. Sarah signs her own consent. p 11

21 December 1786. Peter FOLLIS and Molly Wall. Sur. Charles Walden. Wit. William Peter Martin. p 9

4 March 1796. Adam FOOT and Sarah King. Sur. Joel Clark. p 33

26 June 1800. Peter FORE and Margaret Ward. Sur. Robert Cobbs. Married 28 June by Rev. Thomas Dobson. p 42

23 May 1792. George FOSTER and Allie Turner. Sur. James Howerton. Allie signs her own consent. Married 5 June by Rev. Reuben Pickett. p 25

24 June 1793. Jesse FOSTER and Sarah Ozbrooks. Sur. Hamlett Bolling. p 28

2 March 1788. John FOULKES and Mary Comer. Sur. Moore Comer. Married by Rev. John Atkinson who says <u>Folkes</u>. p 13

9 November 1789. John FOURQUREAN and Mary Farmer, dau. Joel Farmer who consents. Sur. Isaac Easley. Married 12 November by Rev. Hawkins Landrum who says <u>Faurqusin</u>. p 16

31 July 1800. Arthur FOWLER and Sally Douglass, dau. John Douglass who consents. Sur. Joseph Varner. Wit. Epaphroditus Sydnor. Married by Rev. Hawkins Landrum. p 43

21 March 1800. John A. FOWLKES and Nancy Roberts, dau. Michael Roberts, deceased. Sur. Edward Roberts. Wit. Hubert Macke. Consent of William Roberts, guardian of Nancy. Married 26 March by Rev. Alexander Hay. p 44

24 November 1788. Huriah FRANCIS and Jane Carter, dau. John and Sarah Carter who consent. Sur. Micajah Francis. p 13

15 February 1787. John FRANCIS and Elizabeth Scates, dau. Pegey (father) Scates who consents. Sur. Davis Pattey. Wit. Mary Scates. p 11

27 September 1789. Micajah FRANCIS and Elizabeth Francis. Sur. Nathaniel Francis. p 17

7 November 1797. Micajah FRANCIS and Polley Bryan, dau. John Bryan, Sr. who consents. Sur. Nelson Bryan. Wit. John Bryan, Jr. p 35

24 September 1798. Nathaniel FRANCIS and Judy Bond, dau. Philip Bond who consents. Sur. William Gunson. Wit. James Harris. p 39

27 December 1797. William FRANCIS and Anne Adams, dau. John Adams who consents. Sur. Moza Adams. Wit. John Street and John Carter. p 37

12 May 1800. James FRANKLIN and Elizabeth Coates. Sur. William Coates, Sr. Wit. Sarah Bryan. Married 15 May by Rev. Thomas Dobson. p 42

25 December 1793. John FRANKLIN and Rebeckah Younger. Sur. Samuel Younger. Married by Rev. Hawkins Landrum. p 28

27 January 1795. Joseph FRANKLIN and Betsy Nelson. Sur. George Nelson. p 32

7 February 1769. John FREEMAN and Ann Williams. Sur. William Sydnor. Wit. Thomas Tunstall. p 2

26 January 1792. Henry FULFORD and Hannah Jackson. Sur. William Stephens. Hannah signs her own consent. Married by Rev. Thomas Dobson. p 25

18 November 1789. Thomas GAINES and Elizabeth Wall. Sur. Richard Gaines. Elizabeth signs her own consent. Married 23 November by Rev. John Atkinson. p 16

15 May 1770. Charles GALLOWAY and Mary Spragins, dau. Thomas Spragins. Sur. Epaphroditus White. Wit. Thomas Tunstall. p 2

3 March 1789. James GALLOWAY and Elizabeth Spraggins, dau. Thomas Spraggins who consents. Sur. Mel. Spraggins. p 15

8 December 1790. Thomas GARROT and Nancy Bottom, dau. Saley Bottom who consents. Sur. Daniel DeJarnette. p 18

18 October 1787. James GATES and Betty Robertson. Sur. William Gates. p 11

29 June 1799. Robert GEE and Elizabeth Puckett. Sur. Elias Puckett.
p 41

21 August 1792. Shadrack GENTRY and Susanna Daviss, dau. Jonathan and
Bathsheba Daviss who consent. Sur. Meshack Gentry. Married
22 August by Rev. Reuben Pickett. p 25

23 February 1786. Jordan GEORGE and Rosamond Mattox. Married by Rev.
Hawkins Landrum. See Judson George. Ministers' Returns p 21

16 February 1786. Judson GEORGE and Rosamond Maddox, dau. George
Maddox who consents. Sur. Isaac Tynes. Wit. B._____ Maddox. See
Jordan George. p 9

22 November 1791. Richard GEORGE and Tabitha Cheatham. Sur. Isaac
Tynes. Consent of Joel Cheatham for Tabitha; no relationship stated.
p 20

26 August 1779. Joseph GHOLSON and Frankey Waddill, dau. Noel Waddill.
Sur. William Waddill. Wit. William Watkins. p 4

20 October 1782. Daniel GILL and Judith Slaughter, dau. Ezekiel
Slaughter. Sur. John Gill. Wit. Cornelius Cunshaw and Samuel
Slaughter. p 5

29 January 1793. William GLASSCOCK and Betsey Sandford. Kerron Sandford, mother of Betsey, consents. Sur. William Yancy. Married
14 February by Rev. Alexander Hay. p 28

8 September 1798. James GLAZEBROOK and Elizabeth Spence, dau. Margaret
Spence who consents. Sur. James Brown. Wit. William Faulkner. p 40

22 November 1790. Joseph GLENN and Nancy Butler, dau. Joshua Butler
who consents. Sur. George Wiley. Married by Rev. Reuben Pickett.
Returned 18 November.

13 September 1780. William GLENN and Anne Billups. Sur. John Lawson.
Wit. Henry Goare. p 4

19 December 1792. George GODBEE and Nancy Seamore. Married by Rev.
Reuben Pickett. See George Goodbie. Ministers' Returns p 77

11 July 1791. George GODBY and Sarah S. Wall. Sur. John Faulkner.
Sarah signs her own consent. See George Goodby. p 21

25 November 1791. Russell GODBY and Kitty Lacey. Sur. John Pound.
Married 1 December by Rev. Alexander Hay. p 21

19 April 1794. Daniel GOOD and Polly Jones. Sur. Robert Glidwell. Reuben Jones consents for Polly; no relationship stated. p 29

24 June 1793. Thomas GOOD and Susannah Sawyers. Sur. William Combs. Susannah signs her own consent. Married by Rev. John Atkinson. p 27

26 November 1792. George GOODBIE and Nanny Seamans. Sur. Hampton Wade. Nanny signs her own consent. See George Godbee. p 25

13 July 1791. George GOODBY and Sarah Wall. Married by Rev. Reubin Pickett. See George Godby. Ministers' Returns p 54

17 May 1800. Samuel GOODE and Fanny Rowlett, dau. William Rowlett who consents. Sur. William B. Vaughan. Married 29 May by Rev. Thomas Dobson. p 43

15 October 1782. James GOODWIN and Joannah Terry. Sur. Moses Terry. Wit. Henry Goare. p 5

7 July 1784. Richard GOODWIN and Sarah Terry. Sur. Moses Terry. Wit. Henry Goare. p 6

7 January 1789. William GOODWIN and Nancy Abbott. Sur. Robert Trammel. Nancy signs her own consent. Married 12 January by Rev. Hawkins Landrum. p 16

6 May 1756. John GORDON and Isabel Lawson. Sur. James Irwin. Wit. Theophilus Lacy and William Wright. p 1

19 February 1784. Benjamin GORLIN and Candace Burley. Sur. John Black. Wit. Henry Goare. p 6

24 March 1788. Benjamin GOSNELL and Judith Echols, dau. Joseph Echols who consents. Sur. Jeremiah Echols. Wit. Obadiah Echols and A. Echols. p 3

28 January 1800. Elijah GRADY and Betsy Perrin Washburn. Sur. John Washborn. p 42

22 December 1800. Archibald GRANT and Judith Navarre. Sur. John Irvine. p 43

17 November 1794. Charles GRANT and Polly R. Bradshaw, dau. Richard Bradshaw who consents. Sur. William Bradshaw. Married 20 November by Rev. James Watkins. p 29

5 December 1787. Chesley GRANT and Tillethey Kidd. Sur. James Grant. Wit. James Kidd and Anthony Gresham. Tillethey signs her own consent. Married 6 December by Rev. Reuben Pickett. p 11

8 February 1783. Isaac GRANT and Betty Farris. Married by Rev. Nathaniel Hall. Ministers' Returns p 8

28 November 1786. James GRANT and Tabby Kidd. Sur. James Kidd. Wit. William Peter Martin. Married 30 November by Rev. Reuben Pickett. p 9

22 October 1792. Moses GRANT and Elizabeth Grant, dau. Burrell Grant who consents. Sur. James Hill. p 26

11 January 1787. Esom GRAVES and Judith Parrott. Married by Rev. James Watkins. Ministers' Returns p 26

27 November 1786. Reuben GRAVES and Elizabeth Yarborough. Sur. Henry Hopson, Jr. Wit. E. Parrot, John Dial and J. T. Turner. Elizabeth signs her own consent. Married 28 November by Rev. James Watkins. p 9

27 March 1781. William GRAVES and Rebeckah East. Sur. George Vaughan. Wit. Henry Goare. p 5

24 January 1791. Larkin GRAVET and Sally Malone. Sur. Alexander Harrell. Married 27 January by Rev. Reuben Pickett. p 22

6 January 1789. Berryman GREEN and Nancy Terry. Sur. William Terry. p 16

6 October 1796. James GREEN and Patsey Medley, dau. Mehetabelle Medley who consents. Sur. Berryman Green. Wit. Judith Medley. Married 20 October by Rev. Reuben Pickett. p 35

16 December 1789. Peter GREEN and Elizabeth Terry, dau. William Terry who consents. Sur. James Thompson. p 15

20 April 1787. James GREENHILL and Martha Scates. Sur. William Oliver. p 11

20 July 1769. John GREENWOOD and Ann Bates. Sur. Robert Greenwood. p 2

28 November 1790. Beman GREGORY and Judy Gravatt. Sur. William Jones. Judy signs her own consent. Married 2 December by Rev. Reuben Pickett. p 18

24 March 1787. Ambrose GRESHAM and Betty Eppes. Sur. John Eppes. Betty signs her own consent. Married by Rev. Hawkins Landrum. Returned 29 April. p 12

20 January 1794. George GRESHAM and Jane Boyd, dau. James Boyd who consents. Sur. Abner Boyd. Married 29 January by Rev. Reuben Pickett. p 29

2 August 1800. Moses GRESHAM and Elizabeth Boyd. Sur. Jesse Finch. p 43

24 December 1792. Ralph GRESHAM and Hannah Wyatt, dau. William Wyatt who consents. Sur. Major Wyatt. Anthony Gresham consents for Ralph; no relationship stated. John Gresham witnessed the consent. Married 25 December by Rev. Reuben Pickett. p 26

10 January 1799. George GREY and Fanny Brooks. Married by Rev. Reuben Pickett. Ministers' Returns p 137

22 June 1795. James GRIFFIN and Isabel Boyd. Sur. John Boyd. Married by Rev. Samuel D. Brame. p 32

29 October 1788. John GRIFFIN and Sally Parish. Sur. David Parish. Married 1 November by Rev. Henry Lester. p 13

28 January 1793. Spencer GRIFFIN and Sally Townes. Sur. William Griffin. Married by Rev. John Atkinson. p 28

23 July 1799. Nathaniel GUILL and Polley Hughes, dau. John Hughes who consents. Sur. John H. Ligon. Married by Rev. John Ligon. p 41

6 August 1794. William GUILL and Sally Throckmorton. Sur. Robert Throckmorton. Married by Rev. Leonard Baker. p 29

1 May 1794. Hamblin GUNN and Elizabeth Tunstall, dau. John Orvil Tunstall who consents. Sur. Thomas A. Watlington. Wit. Joseph E. Haley and Frankey Haley. Married by Rev. Thomas Dobson. p 29

4 February 1799. William GUNSON and Susannah Harris. Sur. James Harris. p 42

7 June 1786. Cason GUTHREY and Dwithe Reevers. Sur. Joseph Miller. Wit. Obadiah Hendrick. This name is written Carson in other places in the record. p 9

25 July 1798. Nathaniel GUTHRIE and Fanny Link, dau. John Link who consents. Sur. J. Warrin. Wit. Charles Guthrie. p 39

9 October 1789. Bartlett GWINN and Betsy Polley. Sur. William Gates. p 15

30 October 1780. John GWINN and Jeane Wade, dau. John Wade. Sur. David Wade. Wit. Henry Goare. p 4

5 September 1792. Anthony D. HADEN and Patsey Vaughan. Sur. John Owen. Patsey signs her own consent. Married 11 October by Rev. Thomas Dobson who says Hayden. p 25

10 February 1796. Burwell HAGOOD and Sally Irby. Sur. Henry Hagood. Wit. Anthony Irby. Sally signs her own consent. p 34

3 December 1796. Archibald HALEY and Polly Medley, dau. James Medley who consents. Sur. John Orvil Tunstall. Wit. Jency Medley and Lucy Medley. Married by Rev. John Atkinson. Return dated 24 June 1797. p 34

14 November 1800. Lovelace HALEY and Rachel Lamkin, dau. Richard Lamkin who consents. Sur. John Lamkin. Married by Rev. John Atkinson who says Lampkin. p 43

11 August 1788. Richard HALEY and Millycent Hunt. Sur. Joseph E. Haley. She signs her own consent as Millicent. p 14

19 September 1791. Wyatt HALEY and Alice Coles Bennett, dau. Walter Bennett. Sur. Archibald Haley. Married 20 September by Rev. Alexander Hay. p 22

30 December 1794. Edward HALL and Nancy Roberts. Sur. Moses Roberts. p 30

30 August 1787. George HALL and Nancy Watlington. Married by Rev. Hawkins Landrum. Ministers' Returns p 30

8 August 1783. Isham HALL and Juriah Layne. Married by Rev. Nathaniel Hall. Ministers' Returns p 8

18 August 1800. John Robins HALL and Sally Hurt, dau. Philemon Hurt who consents. Sur. Robert Hurt. Wit. Nathaniel Barksdale, Jr. p 45

26 November 1798. Thomas HALL and Polley Yates. Sur. John Yates and Benjamin Hall. Married 20 December by Rev. Thomas Dobson. p 40

25 February 1793. William HALL and Anney Miller. Sur. Harmon Miller. Married 28 February by Rev. Alexander Hay who says Anne. p 28

12 October 1789. William HAMBLETT and Mary Brooks. Married by Rev. William Moore. Ministers' Returns p 44

3 December 1796. John HAMBLIN and Sarah Harrison. Married by Rev. William Moore. Ministers' Returns p 116

- January 1786. Bolling HAMLETT and Polly Combes, dau. George Combes. Sur. William Hamlett. Polly signs her own consent. Married by Rev. William Dodson. p 8

22 February 1786. William HAMLETT and Henrietta Maria Baker, dau. Martin Baker who consents. Sur. Ransom Colquitt. Wit. William Wilson and Reuben Ragland. Married by Rev. James Watkins who says Hamblett and Henrietta Baker. p 9

2 -   1791. Ahab HAMPTON and Nancy Cheatham, dau. David Cheatham. p 21

4 February 1786. Hose (Hoseah?) HAMPTON and Rachel Dotson, dau. William Dotson. Sur. Talmun Haber. Wit. Mary Dudley. See Joseph Hampton. p 8

31 December 1791. Job HAMPTON and Agnes Lawson. Moses Lawson consents for Agnes and is surety; no relationship stated. Married 5 January 1792 by Rev. Jesse Owen. p 20

- December 1785. Joseph HAMPTON and Rachel Dodson. Married by Rev. William Dodson. See Hose Hampton. Ministers' Returns p 17

9 February 1788. David HAMRICK and Letice Wyatt. Sur. John Lawson. Letice signs her own consent. p 14

24 October 1791. Anderson HANCOCK and Jerusha Brumfield. Sur. Barnet Handrake. Wit. Benjamin Hubbard and Nathaniel Hubbard. Benjamin Hubbard signs the certificate. Married 3 November by Rev. Jesse Owen. p 21

6 February 1795. Benjamin HANCOCK and Mary McIntire. Sur. John Charley. Wit. John Carter and Anderson Hancock. Mary signs her own consent. p 32

23 June 1788. John HANCOCK and Elizabeth Turner. Thomas Skates (Scates) consents. (For which one?) p 14

16 December 1785. Joseph HANCOCK and Mary Burchfield, dau. John Burch-field. Sur. John Fisher. Married by Rev. William Dodson. p 7

22 July 1793. Lewis HANCOCK and Nancy Worthey. Sur. Francis M. Petty. Nancy signs her own consent as Nancy Worthy. p 28

9 May 1792. Barnat HANDCOCK and Mary Scates. Sur. William Brumfield. Anderson Handcock signs the certificate of consent; no relationship stated. Married 11 May by Rev. Jesse Owen who says Barnett Hancock and Mary Seats. p 24

24 May 1786. William HANES and Sally McGregger. Sur. Richard Lamkin. Wit. William P. Martin. Married 28 May by Rev. John Atkinson. p 8

13 December 1800. James HANKLEY and Polley West. Sur. Benjamin L. West. p 43

41

13 December 1800. James HANKLEY and Polley West. Sur. Benjamin L. West. p 43

14 March 1796. Thomas HANKLEY and Delphy West. Sur. William West. p 34

27 November 1792. John HANNAH and Sally Finch. Sur. Richard Finch. Married 13 December by Rev. Thomas Dobson. p 25

27 October 1786. Thomas HANSON and Mary Dudley. Married by Rev. James Watkins. Ministers' Returns p 20

14 January 1788. John HARDWICK and Drucilla Hamlett, dau. William Hamlett, Sr. who consents. Sur. Littleberry Hamlett. Married 15 January by Rev. Lawkins Landrum who says <u>Hamblett</u>. p 14

22 January 1798. Lewis HARDWICK and Gillis Walker. Sur. Jesse Owen. Gillis signs her own consent. Married 25 January by Rev. Thomas Dobson. p 40

4 April 1787. William HARDWICK and Sarah Easley. Sur. Warham Easley. Married 5 April by Rev. Hawkins Landrum. p 11

4 December 1785. James HARPER and Agness Burchfield. Sur. John Burch- field. Wit. William P. Martin. Married by Rev. William Dodson. Returns in December. p 7

26 April 1790. John HARPER and Elizabeth Mickelborough. Sur. John Martin. Elizabeth signs her own consent. Married by Rev. John Atkinson. p 18

6 July 1787. Robert HARPER and Lucy Grove. Sur. Elisha Dodson. Lucy signs her own consent. p 11

11 May 1783. Alexander HARRELSON and Mary Malone. This marriage is in the Ministers' Returns by no name is signed. Ministers' Returns p 204

26 August 1800. Burges HARRELSON and Nancy Collins, dau. William Collins who consents. Sur. John Harrelson. Wit. Daniel Collins. Married 28 August by Rev. Reuben Pickett. p 43

4 April 1791. Lea HARRELSON and Mary Stanfield. Sur. William Stan- field. Robert Stanfield consents for Mary; no relationship stated. p 22

6 January 1787. Bernard HARRIS and Anna Askrie or Asksie. Married by Rev. Thomas Dobson. See Brainard Harris. Ministers' Returns p 25

3 December 1786. Brainard HARRIS and Anne Asken, dau. Daniel and Rachel Asken who consent. Sur. Amos Asken. Consent of William and Elizabeth Harris, parents of Brainard. See Bernard Harris. p 8

17 November 1798. Charles T. HARRIS and Tabitha Lovelace, dau. Tabitha Lovelace who consents. Sur. Thomas Lovelace. Wit. Joseph Thompson and William Womack. Married by Rev. John Atkinson. p 40

24 January 1794. Elisha HARRIS and Nancy Lee. Married by Rev. Thomas Dobson. Ministers' Returns p 96

17 May 1800. Humphrey HARRIS and Sally Gildwell. Sur. Robert Gildwell. Married 22 May by Rev. Reuben Pickett. p 43

26 January 1789. Richard HARRIS and Susannah Irby. Sur. James Holt. Susannah signs her own consent. Married by Rev. John Atkinson. p 15

30 March 1779. Thomas HARRIS and Anne Phillips. Sur. Patrick Fitz- gerald. Wit. Henry Goare. Anne signs her own consent. p 4

30 April 1789. Walker HARRIS and Sarah Durrett. Married by Rev. James Watkins. There is a bond in Pittsylvania County is probably this marriage: 20 April 1789; Walker Harris and Leah Durrat; Sur. William Durrat; page 11 original; page 40 my Pittsylvania County Marriages. Ministers' Returns p 39

23 December 1790. Stith HARRISON and Betsy Hoskins. Sur. Nathan Mannin. Consent of James Hoskins for Betsy; no relationship stated. Married 25 December by Rev. Hawkins Landrum. p 19

18 March 1797. Stith HARRISON and Lettice Crutchfield, dau. George Crutchfield who consents. Sur. William Chandler. Married 19 March by Reuben Pickett. p 38

27 October 1786. Thomas HARRISON and Mary Dudley. Sur. Obadiah Harrison. p 9

20 June 1796. Barnard HARRISS and Mary Smallman. Sur. James Brown. Wit. Ruth Brown. Mary signs her own consent. Married 28 June by Rev. Thomas Dobson who says <u>Barnet</u>. p 34

13 March 1789. Ambrose HART and Mary Owen, dau. Joseph Owen who consents. Sur. James Hart. p 15

21 December 1795. Ambrose HART and Judy Barnes. Sur. Jasper Owen. Wit. Bracket Owing. Henry Barnes consents for Judy; no relationship stated. Married by Rev. Samuel D. Brame. p 32

29 December 1800. Ambrose HART and Elizabeth Davis. Sur. William Davis.
p 45

31 December 1798. John HART and Polly Douglass. Sur. Stephen Kent.
Wit. James Davenport. Polly signs her own consent. Married
5 January 1799 by Rev. Leonard Baker. p 40

3 March 1797. John HASELWOOD and Mary Owen. Sur. John Casaday. Mary
signs her own consent. Married by Rev. Thomas Dobson who says
Hazelwood. p 85

9 December 1800. Creed HASKINS and Susannah Watlington, dau. John
Watlington who consents. Sur. Armistead Watlington. Married
11 December by Rev. Alexander Hay. p 43

26 December 1797. John HASKINS and Edna Jones. Sur. Thomas Howerton.
p 37

27 October 1800. Thomas HASKINS and Lucy Jones. Sur. Hampton Jones.
Married 30 October by Rev. Alexander Hay. p 43

30 May 1796. James HATFIELD and Betsey Parker. Sur. William Steel.
Betsey signs her own consent. p 35

26 December 1797. David HAVAL and Nancy Whitehead. Married by Rev.
Hawkins Landrum. Ministers' Returns p 208

28 June 1790. John HAWKINS and Jane Ferguson, dau. Jane Ferguson who
consents. Sur. John Ferguson. p 18

- -   1799. Stokley HAYDEN and Nancy Dodson. Married by Rev. John
Atkinson. Ministers' Returns p 140

20 March 1798. William HAYNES and Elizabeth Vaughan. Sur. Samuel
Landrum. Elizabeth signs her own consent. Married 5 April by Rev.
Hawkins Landrum. p 40

HAZELWOOD see HASELWOOD

16 February 1786. William HEARING and Mary Powel (Powell). Sur. James
Legrand. Mary signs her own consent. See William Herrin. p 10

26 August 1793. Martin HEMPERLY and Rachael Powell. Sur. Adam Foot.
Wit. Edward Powell and John Patterson. Rachael signs her own consent.
Married 5 September by Rev. Alexander Hay. p 27

25 July 1790. Daniel HENDERSON and Ann Clardy, dau. Michael Clardy who
consents. Sur. Thomas Clardy. Married by Rev. William Moore. p 19

6 October 1798. Thomas HENSHAW and Sally Taylor. Sur. William Taylor. Wit. Dudley Taylor. Sally signs her own consent. p 40

16 February 1786. William HERRIN and Mary Powell. Married by Rev. Hawkins Landrum. See William Hearing. Ministers' Returns p 21

27 June 1791. Armistead HERRING and Elizabeth Huddleston, dau. Benjamin Huddleston who consents. Sur. Stephen Herring. Married by Rev. John Atkinson. p 20

10 December 1790. John HEWELL and Elisore Collins. Married by Rev. Reuben Pickett. Ministers' Returns p 62

30 September 1799. Joseph HEWELL and Susanna Ragland, dau. John Ragland who consents. Sur. Roy Boyd. Married 3 October by Rev. Alexander Hay. p 42

26 November 1792. Wyatt HEWELL and Frances Davenport. Sur. William Hewell. Frances signs her own consent. Married 18 December by Rev. Reuben Pickett. p 24

14 June 1792. Larkin HICKERSON and Betsy Cathasin. Married by Rev. Alexander Hay. See Larkin Higgason. Ministers' Returns p 71

28 May 1798. David HICKS and Nancy Childress. Sur. James Watkins. Wit. Joseph Hicks. Consent of Peter and Susanna Crews for Nancy Childress; no relationship stated. Peter Crews m. Susanna Childress 24 June 1797. Married 29 May by Rev. James Watkins. p 40

20 November 1798. Moses HICKS and Susanna Childress. Sur. James Watkins. Wit. John Carmical. Consent of Susanna Crews for Susanna Childress; no relationship stated. Peter Crews m. Susanna Childress 24 June 1797. Married 27 November by Rev. James Watkins. p 40

27 September 1787. Thomas HICKS and Elizabeth Taylor. Married by Rev. James Watkins. See Thomas Hix. Ministers' Returns p 28

7 October 1800. William HICKS and Alcey Dews, dau. John Dews who consents. Sur. Reuben Dews. Wit. William Collins. p 43

13 June 1792. Larkin HIGGASON and Betsy Cothron. Sur. Holcombe Robertson. See Larkin Hickerson. p 24

25 April 1799. Ephraim HILL and Elizabeth Stevens. Sur. John Roberts. Elizabeth signs her own consent. p 42

16 March 1775. James HILL and Sarah Williams, dau. John Williams. Sur. Paul Carrington. Wit. Thomas Fuqua. p 3

17 September 1798. James HILL and Delphy Penticost. Sur. John Penticost. Married 18 September by Rev. Thomas Dobson. p 40

1 July 1799. John HILL and Judah Scurlock, dau. Thomas Scurlock who consents. Sur. Dudley Scurlock. Wit. Nimrod Farguson. p 41

27 June 1796. Joseph HILL and Milley Boyd. Sur. Thomas Boyd. Married by Rev. John Atkinson. p 34

25 April 1791. Robert HILL and Pattey Jones. Sur. Peter Wilson. Married 28 April by Rev. James Watkins. p 22

20 March 1793. Thomas HILL and Mary Forsith. Sur. Armistead Abbott. Wit. Elisha Abbott. Mary signs her own consent. Married 26 March by Rev. Hawkins Landrum who says <u>Parrish</u>. p 27

4 January 1774. William HILL and Marth Dudgson. Sur. Ephraim Hill. Wit. Henry Goare and M_____ Carrington. This is the original bond. See William Veice. p 3

20 July 1788. Zachariah HILL and Sally Mason, dau. Thomas Mason who consents. Sur. John Jones. Married 31 July by Rev. James Watkins who says <u>Sarah</u> Mason. p 14

22 October 1792. James HITTE and Polly Grant, dau. Burrell Grant who consents. Sur. Moses Grant. p 24

20 November 1786. Alexander HITTSON and Rhoda Dodson. Sur. William Dodson. Wit. Thomas and Rhoda Dodson. p 10

22 September 1787. Thomas HIX and Elizabeth Taylor. Sur. William Gregory. Wit. James Watkins and Joseph Hix. Elizabeth signs her own consent. See Thomas Hicks. p 12

24 November 1783. Henry HOBSON and Polly Pate, dau. Jeremiah Pate. Sur. Matthew Pate. Wit. Burrell Grant, Johthan Hobson and John Salmon. p 6

17 September 1778. Joseph HOBSON and Sarah Boyd. Sur. George Boyd, Jr. Gent. p 3

19 May 1772. Nicholas HOBSON and Jane Hobson. Sur. Jonathan Patterson, Jr. Wit. William Taylor. p 2

14 April 1792. Fleming HODGES and Betsy Powell. Sur. Edward Powell. Married by Rev. Hawkins Landrum who says <u>Hodge</u>. Returned 17 May. p 24

21 September 1798. Thomas HODGES and Kesiah Hawkins, dau. Zachariah Hawkins who consents. Sur. John Hawkings. Wit. James Priddy. p 40

24 June 1800. Richard A. HOLLAND and Nancy Chappell. Sur. Joel Chappell. Married 3 July by Rev. Hawkins Landrum. p 43

17 March 1800. Whitfield HOLLOWAY and Henrietta Mitchell. Sur. John Mitchell. Wit. Fanny Word. Consent of Henry Mitchell for Henrietta; no relationship stated. Married by Rev. Nathaniel Holloway. p 43

16 November 1792. John HOLT and Elizabeth Blackwell. Sur. Moses Blackwell. Married by Rev. Thomas Dobson. p 26

27 March 1769. Joseph HOLT and Judith Hall, dau.-in-law B. Wooding. Sur. Simon Holt. Wit. John Byrn and Thomas Tunstall. Does this mean step-daughter? p 2

16 November 1795. Peter HOLT and Pashey Eastes. Sur. Laban Eastes. Pashey signs her own consent. p 32

2 January 1797. William HOLT and Salley Dillard, dau. Richard Dillard who consents. Sur. Benjamin Hall. Sally also signed the certificate. Married 5 January by Rev. Nathaniel Holloway. p 38

13 January 1783. Richard HOOPER and Elizabeth Word. Married by Rev. Nathaniel Hall. Ministers' Returns p 10

25 June 1792. Thomas HOPE and Lucy Pankey. Sur. Francis Day. Wit. Stephen Pankey and Morgan Pankey. Lucy signs her own consent. Married 27 June by Rev. William Moore. p 24

26 December 1796. Edmund HOSKINS and Sarah Fontaine. Sur. Joseph Hopson. Consent of Joseph Fontaine for Sarah; no relationship stated. Married 27 December by Rev. Reuben Pickett. p 34

18 October 1780. James HOSKINS and Mary Sanford. Sur. Robert Sanford. Wit. Henry Goare. p 4

4 August 1773. Samuel HOSKINS and Susanna Watkins, dau. George Watkins. Sur. _____der Gordon. Wit. William Hopkins and Thomas Watkins. p 3

16 February 1786. Wyatt HOWELL and Sally Atkisson, dau. Jesse Atkisson who consents. Sur. John Wood. Wit. William Adkerson and Patrick Boyd. Married by Rev. Reuben Pickett who says Atkerson. Returned 27 July. p 9

27 December 1785. George HOWERTON and Frances Jones. Married by Rev. Reuben Pickett. Ministers' Returns p 12

2 February 1789. James HOWERTON and Nancy Foster. Sur. George Foster. Nancy signs her own consent. Married by Rev. Reuben Pickett. p 15

24 November 1785. Thomas HOWERTON and Frances Jones. Sur. Johnson Faulkner. Frances signs her own consent. p 7

7 April 1786. Benjamin HUBBARD and Susanna Gillenton. Sur. Mons. Hendrick. Wit. Moses Hendrick, James Echols and Elizabeth Martin. p 9

8 October 1791. Benjamin HUBBARD and Mary Worsham. Sur. Samuel Hubbard. Wit. James Martin. Mary signs her own consent. Married 13 October by Rev. Jesse Owen. p 22

26 January 1795. Moses HUBBARD and Sarah Wood. Sur. Patrick Brady. Wit. William Haynes. Sarah signs her own consent. Married 5 February by Rev. Hawkins Landrum. p 32

15 April 1799. Robert HUBBARD and Polly Winfrey, dau. Charles Winfrey who consents. Sur. Jacob Amonett. Wit. William Hubbard and Samuel Hubbard. p 42

31 October 1791. Samuel HUBBARD and Patience Hurt, dau. William Hurt who consents. Sur. John Adams. p 23

23 December 1793. Stephen HUDDLESTON and Sarah Coates. Sur. Philip Carter. Married 26 January by Rev. Thomas Dobson. p 27

18 January 1798. Daniel HUDSON and Francis Camp, dau. John Camp who consents. Sur. George Camp. Married 19 January by Rev. Thomas Dobson. p 40

22 December 1794. Hill HUDSON and Polley Owen, dau. Ambrose Owen who consents. Sur. Champion Owen. Wit. Daniel Owen. p 30

7 April 1783. Daniel HUGHES and Nancy Briggs. This marriage is in the Ministers' Returns but no name is signed. Ministers' Returns p 204

18 March 1774. John HUGHES and Lucy Irby. Sur. Armistead Watlington. Wit. Paul Carrington. p 3

26 December 1796. Joseph HUGHES and Ann Munday. Sur. Absalom Hughes. Married 28 December by Rev. Reuben Pickett. p 34

9 May 1796. Robert HUGHES and Sally Brent. Sur. Samuel Davis. Sally signs her own consent. p 34

2 January 1788. Stephen HUGHES and Tabitha Finch. Sur. Richard Finch. p 14

1 December 1791. Elijah HUNDLEY and Lucrettia Edy Mackey. Sur. Thomas Dobson. Married by Rev. Thomas Dobson. p 20

13 September 1781. John HUNDLEY and Keziah Sims. Sur. Shadrack East. Keziah signs her own consent. p 5

25 June 1798. Benjamin HUNT and Susanna Roberts. Married by Rev. Leonard Baker. Ministers' Returns p 133

6 December 1800. George HUNT and Polley Adams, dau. (?) Thomas Powell who consents. Sur. Philip Adams. Wit. George Collins. Was Thomas Powell Polley's step-father? Married 11 December by Rev. Reuben Pickett. p 43

19 December 1781. Gilbert HUNT and Susannah Martin. Sur. John Wimbish. Wit. Henry Goare. p 5

20 December 1787. James HUNT and Rhoda Nunnally. Sur. Daniel Roberts. Rhoda signs her own consent. p 11

9 March 1754. Memican HUNT and Mary Wade. Sur. Robert Hunt. Out of place, should be on p 1. p 194

15 May 1753. Nathaniel HUNT and Elizabeth Wade. Sur. Andrew Wade. Wit. James Foulis and Robert Wade. p 1

15 September 1785. Thomas HUNT and Molly Bruice (Bruce). Sur. Michael Bruce. Married by Rev. Thomas Dobson who says Bruis. Returned 8 December. p 7

13 November 1788. David HUNTER and Dorcas Shelton, dau. Charleston Shelton who consents. Sur. Owen Thomas. Wit. Cabell C. Dodson. Married by Rev. John Atkinson. p 14

26 August 1794. Anderson HURST and Mary Medley, dau. Joseph Medley who consents. Sur. John Irvine. Wit. David Brandon. p 29

23 July 1798. Anderson I. HURST and Elizabeth Pointer, dau. Samuel Pointer who consents. Sur. Nathaniel Jones. Wit. Kemp Hurst. p 40

20 June 1782. James HURT and Agness Harrison. Sur. Philamon Hurt. Wit. Phoebe Hurt, Moza Hurt and Henry Goare. Agness signs her own consent. p 5

6 December 1786. James HURT and Elizabeth Morris, dau. William Morris. Sur. Talmon Harber. Wit. Joseph Hix. Married 7 December by Rev. James Watkins. p 9

18 April 1782. Moza HURT and Phoebe Mann. Sur. Philamon Hurt. Wit. Henry Goare. Phobe signs her own consent. p 5

2 January 1786. Daniel HUTCHESON and Eliza Johnson. Sur. Charles Kennon. Married 5 January by Rev. Thomas Dobson who says Elizabeth. p 10

4 July 1798. Robert INNES and Tabitha Boyd. Sur. George Boyd. Wit. Joshua Boyd and J. W. Burwell. Tabitha signs her own consent. Married 5 December by Rev. Alexander Hay. p 40

18 November 1774. Charles IRBY and Susanna Ibry. Sur. Thomas Tunstall. Wit. Edmond Tunstall and Mary Tunstall. p 3

8 December 1773. Harrison IRBY and Mary Irby. Sur. Anthony Irby. Wit. Thomas Tunstall. p 3

11 July 1795. Harrison IRBY and Elizabeth Long. Sur. Henry Thomas. Wit. Henry Thomas, Jr. Elizabeth signs her own consent. p 32

20 December 1787. John IRBY and Sarah Whitworth. Sur. Bartlett Crenshaw. Mrs. Sarah Whitworth signs the consent. Was she Sarah's mother or was Sarah a widow? I think she was a widow. Sarah Cunningham m. John Whitworth 15 April 1782. Married 29 December by Rev. Hawkins Landrum. p 11

7 March 1789. John IRBY and Anne Kendrick. Sur. Joshua Irby. Wit. William Kendrick and Benjamin Dawson. She signs her own consent as Anney. Married 10 March by Rev. William Moore. p 15

11 August 1799. Nathaniel IBRY and Patsey Osborn, dau. Samuel Osborn who consents. Sur. William Powell. Married by Rev. Thomas Dobson. p 42

16 March 1790. Samuel IRBY and Nancy Stewart, dau. John Stewart who consents. Sur. David Neely. p 19

23 November 1795. William IRBY and Ann Williams, dau. Luke Williams who consents. Sur. Edmond Irby. Wit. Samuel Irby. Married by Rev. Samuel D. Brame. p 32

15 October 1797. Alexander IRVINE and Mildred McCraw, dau. James McCraw who consents and is surety. Wit. James McCraw, Jr. and Isaac Medley. Married 19 October by Rev. Hawkins Landrum. p 37

1 January 1785. Christopher IRVIN and Prudence Echols, dau. John Echols. Sur. James Chappell. Wit. Henry Goare. p 7

26 December 1791. James IRVINE and Mary Malone. Sur. David Brandon. Mary signs her own consent. Married 29 December by Rev. James Watkins. p 20

1 April 1773. John IRVINE and Elizabeth Lawson, dau. John and Priscilla Lawson who consent. Wit. Thomas Hurst and James Irvine. Consent only. p 3

6 April 1775. John IRVINE and Elizabeth Lawson. Sur. Alexander Irvine. Wit. Paul Carrington. p 3

10 March 1800. Abel JACKSON and Sally Conner. Sur. Ephraim Jackson. Wit. Jesse Owen and William Owen. Sally signs her own consent. p 43

22 October 1787. Hezekiah JACKSON and Alice Shelton. Sur. Owen Decker. Wit. Elizabeth Shelton and Haner Shelton. Alice signs her own consent. p 12

6 March 1791. Bartlett JAMES and Sally Rolings, dau. John and Sally Rolings who consent. Sur. George James. Wit. Edmund May, William Johnson and John James. Bartlett son of Huke Thomas James. p 21

18 October 1786. Hugh F. JAMES and Milly Bryan. Married by Rev. Thomas Dobson. Ministers' Returns p 24

31 January 1791. Peter JARROTT and Susannah Griffin. Sur. John Griffin. p 21

28 October 1791. Atha (Arthur?) JENKINS and Elizabeth Hamblin. Sur. Thomas Hamlin. Married 30 October by Rev. Thomas Dobson who says Artha. p 20

26 December 1794. Gentry JENKINS and Susanna Hamblin. Sur. William Johnson. Wit. William Roberts and Joe Roberts. Consent of Mack (or Mark) and Mary Hamblin for Susanna; no relationship stated. p 31

6 August 1798. Robert JESSUP and Frances Carter. Sur. Richard Carter. Married 9 August by Rev. Hawkins Landrum. p 38

6 October 1787. Charles JINKINS and Winea Burchett, dau. Mary Burchett who consents. Sur. Benjamin Daniel. p 12

3 January 1782. David JOHNSON and Mary Barksdale. Married by Rev. Nathaniel Hall. Ministers' Returns p 10

17 January 1798. Gregory JOHNSON and Elizabeth Henderson, dau. Charles Henderson who consents. Sur. Philip Johnson. Wit. Isham Palmer. p 40

6 August 1793. Morris JOHNSON and Sally Fleming. Sur. William Fleming. Married 8 August by Rev. Thomas Dobson. p 28

27 January 1798. Philip JOHNSON and Betsy Watkins, dau. Thomas Watkins who consents. Sur. Gregory Johnson. p 40

21 December 1784. Richard JOHNSON and Frances Phelps. Married by Rev. Nathaniel Hall. Ministers' Returns p 204

4 June 1789. Solomon JOHNSON and Sarah Morris. Married by Rev. James Watkins. Ministers' Returns p 39

12 July 1786. Thomas JOHNSON and Barbara Hutcheson, dau. David Hutcheson who consents. Sur. James Johnson. Wit. Obadiah Hendrick. Married by Rev. James Watkins. p 9

21 January 1794. Thomas JOHNSON and Penelope Hardwick. Sur. Adam Foot. Married 23 January by Rev. Reuben Pickett. p 31

2 June 1787. William JOHNSON and Amey Jinkins, dau. John Jinkins who consents. Sur. David Adams. Wit. Thomas Dobson. p 12

11 November 1794. Jeremiah JOHNSTON and Bitsey Thaxton. Sur. William Boxley. Consent of William Thaxton for Bitsey; no relationship stated. p 31

15 February 1792. Daniel JONES and Catherine Lee. Sur. Thomas Watts. Wit. Samuel Watts. William Lee consents for Catherine; no relation-ship stated. Married 16 February by Rev. Thomas Dobson. p 24

12 April 1800. David JONES and Bethany Hedgpeth. Sur. Nathan Jones. Wit. Samuel Hedgpeth and Edmond Holloway. Bethany signs her own consent. Married 14 April by Rev. Elias Dodson. p 43

12 July 1790. George JONES and Anne Jones. Sur. William Jones. Wit. Jesse Barnes. Anne signs her own consent. p 19

14 January 1794. Gutruth JONES and Mary Whitt. Sur. William Whitt. Mary signs her own consent. Married 15 January by Rev. Reuben Pickett who says Gutrick. p 30

23 February 1795. James JONES and Winnifred Watkins. Sur. Philip Vass. Wit. Alexander Vass. Winnifred signs her own consent. Married 25 February by Rev. James Watkins. p 32

1 September 1798. John JONES and Darkness Allen. Sur. Nathaniel Douglas. Wit. Thomas Jones. Darkness signs her own consent. p 40

6 December 1788. John JONES and Sally Gunter. Sur. John Hughes. p 14

2 November 1792. John JONES and Nancy Pendergrass, dau. Richard Pendergrass who consents. Sur. Nathan Jones. p 24

15 April 1800. Nathan JONES and Elizabeth Anderson. Married by Rev. Elias Dodson. Ministers' Returns p 146

26 September 1791. Nathaniel JONES and Judith Pointer, dau. Samuel Pointer. Sur. William Thompson. p 21

26 March 1799. Robert JONES and Barbara Wyatt, dau. John Wyatt who consents and is surety. Wit. John Wyatt, Jr. Married 27 March by Rev. Thomas Dobson. p 42

16 August 1800. Robert JONES and Patsy McComack. Sur. Nathan Jones. Wit. John Jones. Patsy signs her own consent. Married 19 August by Rev. Elias Dodson. p 43

29 October 1788. Stephen JONES and Elizabeth Trevilion. Sur. John Griffin. Wit. David Parrish. Elizabeth signs her own consent. Married 1 November by Rev. Henry Lester who says Trevelein. p 12

21 March 1792. Thomas JONES and Lucy Whitton. Sur. William Flin. Wit. William Moseley. Lucy signs her own consent. Married by Rev. Thomas Dobson who says Whitlaw. p 24

13 December 1797. Thomas JONES and Elizabeth Osborne Moseley, dau. Blackman Moseley who consents. Sur. Morton Clay. Wit. Joseph Faulkner. p 37

25 March 1792. Thomas JONES and Lucy Whitlaw. Married by Rev. Thomas Dobson. Ministers' Returns p 88

23 December 1800. William JONES and Polly Stephens, dau. William Stephens who consents. Sur. Henry Stephens. Wit. Sally Stephens. Married 27 December by Rev. John Ligon. p 43

17 January 1781. Anthony JUANELL and Obedience Cockerham. Married by Rev. Thomas Dobson. Ministers' Returns p 204

16 December 1789. Robert JUNIEL and Sally Douglass. Sur. Robert Allen. Wit. Memucan Allen and Andrew Juniel. Sally signs her own consent. p 15

27 July 1767. Richard KEARBY and Esther Anderson, dau. Richard Anderson. Sur. John Lawson. Wit. Jacob Sheppard and John Anderson. p 2

9 July 1799. Edmund KEELING and Nancy Francis. Sur. Nathaniel Francis. p 42

10 February 1797. Francis KEELING and Elizabeth Francis. Sur. Vincent Francis. Elizabeth signs her own consent. p 37

20 October 1784. Thomas KEELING and Nancy Fleet. Married by Rev. Nathaniel Hall. Ministers' Returns p 204

6 December 1794. Thomas KEELING and Mildred Pillars. Sur. Thomas Skates. Wit. William Brumfield and Daniel Dejarnett. p 31

2 August 1793. William KEEN and Polly Pleasants. Sur. William Thompson. Married 8 August by Rev. Drury Craig. p 26

27 December 1790. Peter Field KENT and Elizabeth Hill, dau. Elizabeth Hill who consents. Sur. James Thompson. Married 30 December by Rev. Alexander Hay. p 19

6 March 1797. Jeremiah KERBY and Esther Anderson, dau. Meades Anderson (father) who consents. Sur. John Anderson. Married 9 March by Rev. Lawkins Landrum. p 37

18 April 1791. Richard KERBY and Alice Anderson, dau. Meades Anderson who consents. Sur. John Anderson. Married 21 April by Rev. Hawkins Landrum who says Kirby. p 23

28 -   1786. James KIDD and Mourning Hicks. Sur. James Grant. Wit. William Peter Martin. p 9

21 May 1792. Henry KING and Nancy Smith. Sur. Thomas Tune. Married 30 May by Rev. Jesse Owen. p 24

25 February 1789. Robert KING and Sally Lacy. Sur. Matthew Lacy. Thomas Lacy consents for Sally; no relationship stated. Married 4 March by Rev. Hawkins Landrum. p 15

14 November 1799. William KING and Elizabeth Gill. Married by Rev. Hawkins Landrum. Ministers' Returns p 144

1 May 1800. William KING and Polley Torian. Sur. Scare Torian. Wit. John Faulkes. Consent of Thomas Torian, guardian of Polley. Married by Rev. Alexander Hay. p 43

19 December 1786. John KIRBY and Orpha Anderson. Sur. John Pettit. Wit. William Peter Martin. Richard Anderson consents for Orpha; no relationship stated. Married 21 December by Rev. Hawkins Landrum who says Apha. p 9

19 December 1791. Obadiah KIRBY and Ruth Hendrick dau. Moses Hendrick who consents. Married 22 December by Rev. Hawkins Landrum who says Kerby. p 21

2 September 1784. John LACY and Alice Sydnor. Sur. Robert D. R. Milner. Wit. Henry Goare. Married 15 September by Rev. Nathaniel Hall. p 6

54

20 January 1795. Absalom LAIN and Polley Guttrey, dau. Travis Guttrey who consents. Sur. William Lain. Wit. William Guttrey. p 33

23 March 1789. John LAMPKIN and Anne Farguson, dau. Jane Farguson who consents. Sur. Thomas Jeffress. p 15

22 October 1798. Joseph LANDRUM and Elizabeth Dickson. Sur. Benjamin Dickson. Married 28 October by Rev. Hawkins Landrum. p 39

21 December 1786. David LANE and Rachel Gosneill. Sur. Benjamin Gosneill, written Goswell and changed to Gosneill. p 10

7 October 1797. John LANE and Mary Watts Mullins. Sur. David D. Mullins. p 37

11 November 1795. William LANKESTER and Susanna Martin, dau. William Martin who consents. Sur. Nathaniel Bates. Wit. Isaac Gregory. p 33

- January 1771. Benjamin LANKFORD and Henrica Booker. Sur. Epaphroditus White. Wit. William Merriwether. p 2

3 October 1794. David LAWSON and Winney Dottson. Sur. Hosai (Hosea?) Hampton. Wit. Thomas Ward. Winney signs her own consent. Married 12 October by Rev. Thomas Dobson who says Winney Dobson. p 31

- February 1791. Francis LAWSON and Betsy Taylor, dau. Charles Taylor. Sur. John Lawson. p 22

18 December 1778. John LAWSON and Martha Bates. Sur. John Brandon. Wit. Henry Goare. Martha signs her own consent. p 3

19 February 1782. John LAWSON and Anne Irvine. Sur. Alexander Irvine. Wit. Henry Goare. p 6

24 April 1786. John LAWSON and Elizabeth Miller. Sur. William Pearman. Elizabeth signs her own consent. p 8

26 September 1800. Peter LAWSON and Hannah Fulford. Sur. James Wilkinson. p 43

4 January 1782. Thomas LAWSON and Hannah Fuqua. Joseph Fuqua, Sr. guardian of Hannah consents. Sur. John Moore. Wit. Henry Goare. p 5

24 May 1758. William LAWSON and Jane Banks. Sur. George Bays. p 1

21 November 1786. Timothy LAX and Sistyry Murphy. Sur. John Lax. Wit.
Thomas Puckett and John Lewis. Gives her own consent by her mark.
Married 23 November by Rev. Thomas Dobson who says <u>Sistissery</u>. p 8

27 January 1794. William LAX and Fanny Swinny. Sur. Benjamin Swinny.
Married by Rev. Samuel D. Brame. p 31

21 February 1789. John LEA and Mary (Sally written over it) McCarty.
Married by Rev. James Watkins. Ministers' Returns p 39

22 January 1798. George LEAGUE and Nancy Morris. Sur. Ephraim Jackson.
Wit. Matthew Malcom. Nancy signs her own consent. p 38

11 January 1794. Joseph LEE and Sally Werly. This is in the Ministers'
Returns by not signed by a minister. Instead it is marked "Teste :
George Carrington, Clerk." Name spelled Worley in another copy.
Ministers' Returns p 100

20 November 1763. James LEGRAND, Gent. and Betty Wade. Sur. Hampton
Wade. p 1

17 April 1779. John LEGRAND and Elizabeth Younger. Sur. Alexander
Gordon. Wit. Henry Goare. p 3

20 February 1783. Charles LEWIS and Joice Price, dau. William Price.
Sur. Luke Williams. Wit. William B. Price and William Irby. p 6

27 December 1785. Edward LEWIS and Nancy Price, dau. William and Mary
Price who consent. Sur. William Hobson. Wit. Charles Lewis.
Married by Rev. William Dodson. p 7

29 April 1789. John LEWIS and Milly Cannady, dau. William Cannady who
consents and is surety. p 15

2 February 1776. Nicholas LEWIS, Gent and Elizabeth Meriwether, dau.
Thomas Meriwether. Sur. Thomas Tunstall. Wit. William Meriwether
and John Lewis, father of Nicholas. p 3

24 June 1795. Robert LEWIS and Anna Ragland. Sur. Paul Watlington.
Wit. Evan Ragland, Sr. Anna signs her own consent. Married 25 June
by Rev. Alexander Hay. p 33

27 August 1774. John LIGHT, JR. and Joanna Dixon. Sur. George
Watkins. p 3

4 July 1793. William LIGHT and Dolly Younger. Sur. Samuel Younger.
Dolly signs her own consent. Married 6 July by Rev. Hawkins Landrum.
p 27

17 January 1782. Blackman LIGON and Elizabeth Townes. Sur. Henry Townes. Wit. Henry Goare. p 6

11 June 1789. James LIGON and Judith Church. Sur. Joseph Ligon. Judith signs her own consent. Married 25 June by Rev. Henry Lester. p 15

12 November 1782. John LIGON and Nancy Anderson Martin, dau. George Martin. Sur. John Norris. Wit. Moses Harrison and Stephen Wade. p 5

10 June 1784. Joseph LIGON and Lettice Sims. Sur. William Thompson. Wit. George Carrington. p 6

10 April 1790. Joseph LIGON and Diana Coleman Clay. Sur. Coleman Williams. Consent of John William for Diana. p 18

16 October 1799. Obediah LIGON and Anna Isbell. Married by Rev. Reuben Pickett. Ministers' Returns p 137

15 October 1798. Richard H. LIGON and Gincey Wilbourn. Sur. Thomas Wilbourn. Wit. Judah Wilbourn. Married 18 October by Rev. Thomas Dobson who says <u>Jincy</u>. p 39

17 September 1796. John LINCAN and Jemima Hodges. Sur. William Hodges. p 34

23 January 1797. Byrd B. LINK and Susanna Turner, dau. William Turner who consents. Sur. James Warren. Married by Rev. Nathaniel Holloway. p 37

12 December 1789. Thomas LINK and Judy Wilson. Married by Rev. James Watkins. Ministers' Returns p 40

1 October 1799. John LIPSCOMB and Dicey Scott, dau. Dicey Sikes who consents. Sur. James Sikes. Dicey Scott m. Jonas Sikes 7 November 1794. Married 3 October by Rev. James Watkins. p 42

18 March 1779. Thomas LIPSCOMB and Gilley Whitlock. Sur. Thomas Whitlock. Wit. Henry Goare. p 4

24 August 1791. James LITHGO and Lucy Holt. Sur. Martin True. Married 3 September by Rev. Reuben Pickett. p 23

17 August 1790. William LOFTIS and Lucy Conell. Married by Rev. James Watkins. Ministers' Returns p 49

20 December 1787. William LOGAN and Nancy Sidnor. Sur. William Sidnor. p 12

23 March 1789. Isaiah LONDON and Elizabeth Dunkley. Sur. Henry Dunkley.
p 15

14 November 1789. John LONDON and Jane Clardy. Sur. Michael Clardy.
p 15

7 January 1795. Owen LONDON and Elizabeth Whitlow. Sur. John London.
Elizabeth signs her own consent. p 33

27 July 1789. Charles LOVELACE and Rhoda Hart. Sur. Isaac Farguson.
p 16

1 February 1783. William LOVELACE and Sally Fambrough. Married by Rev.
Nathaniel Hall. Ministers' Returns p 8

17 December 1798. Dabney LOWRY and Nancy Hughes. Sur. Jacob Lowry.
Wit. William Faulkner. Nancy signs her own consent. Married
20 December by Rev. James Watkins. p 38

25 March 1799. Jacob LOWRY and Patsey Gholson, dau. Joseph Gholson who
consents. Sur. James Watkins. Wit. Ann Watkins. Married 28 March
by Rev. James Watkins. p 42

15 December 1788. James LOYD and Sarah Chissum, dau. Barbara Chissum
who consents. Sur. Edmond Chissum.   p 14

21 October 1796. Nathaniel LUCK and Dicey Waller. Sur. Richard Waller.
p 34

24 December 1790. Joseph LUCK and Tabitha Harris. Married by Rev.
Hawkins Landrum. Ministers' Returns p 65

17 November 1791. Richard H. LUCK and Betsy Mackalester, dau. William
Mackalester. Sur. Nathaniel Luck. This name is McAlester. p 22

22 April 1789. John LUMPKIN and Anne Ferguson. Married by Rev.
William Moore. Ministers' Returns p 44

1 November 1784. Robert LUMPKIN and Elizabeth Forest. Married by Rev.
Nathaniel Hall. Ministers' Returns p 204

10 August 1799. Jacob LUSTER and Rebecca Wyatt, dau. John Wyatt who
consents and is surety. Married 15 August by Rev. Thomas Dobson.
p 42

4 January 1785. Capt. William LYNCH and Anne Stone. Sur. Thomas Carter.
Wit. Henry Goare. p 7

28 March 1791. John McALESTER and Sally Barley. Sur. John Barley.
Married by Rev. Hawkins Landrum who says McAllister and Boxley. p 23

24 October 1791. James MC ALLESTER and Anne DeJarnette. Sur. John McAllester. p 22

26 December 1791. John MC CANN and Mary Lowry, dau. John Lowry. Sur. Francis Petty. Wit. Joseph Gholson and Carson Guthrey. Married by Rev. James Watkins. Returned 19 January 1792. p 22

22 July 1793. Charles MC CARTY and Ursula Palmer. Sur. James Palmer. Ursula signs her own consent. p 28

13 February 1798. John MC CARTY and Sally Torian. Sur. Joseph Ayres. Wit. Scare (?) Torian. Consent of Thomas Torian for Sally; no relationship stated. Married 22 February by Rev. James Watkins. p 39

30 March 1792. Joseph MC CARTY and Sally Faulkner. Sur. Hampton Wade. Sally signs her own consent. p 25

6 February 1797. John C. MC CRAW and Elizabeth Sydner. Sur. John Lacy. p 37

2 May 1791. William MC CRAW and Mathey Lumpkin. Sur. Robert Lumpkin. Mathey signs her own consent. Married 12 May by Rev. Jesse Owen who says Lampkins. p 22

22 February 1796. William MC CRAW and Jannie Towles Medley. Sur. David Brandon. Jannie signs her own consent. Married 25 February by Rev. Reuben Pickett who says Jane T. p 34

18 August 1773. Johnson MC DANIEL and Elizabeth Maybury. Sur. Obadiah Echols. Wit. William Parr. Johnson son of William McDaniel. p 3

9 February 1792. John MC DOWELL and Polly Brown, dau. Frederick Brown who consents. Sur. Anthony Griffin. Married by Rev. John Atkinson. p 24

28 December 1792. William MC GRIGG and Mary Arnold. Sur. William Arnold. Married 29 December by Rev. Alexander Hay. p 24

12 March 1795. William MC GRIGG and Jemimah Jent. Sur. Abraham Tucker. Wit. Charles Allen and Thomas Lasy (Probably Lacy.) p 33

10 Daniel 1782. Terry MC HANEY and Sarah Luke. Married by Rev. Nathaniel Hall. Ministers' Returns p 10

9 December 1795. James MC KENNEY and Lucy Hurst. Sur. Anderson Hurst. Lucy signs her own consent. Married 14 December by Rev. James Watkins. p 31

23 February 1786. Andrew MC MAHAN and Mary Dillon. Married by Rev.
Hawkins Landrum. See Andrew McMahaney. Ministers' Returns p 21

16 November 1786. Andrew MC MAHANEY and Mary Dillon, dau. Henry Dillon
who consents. See Andrew McMahan. p 8

26 May 1785. Donald MC NICOLL and Susannah Yuille. Sur. James Fletcher.
Wit. Thomas Murdock. Susannah signs her own consent. p 7

MACLIN see MACKLING

11 February 1790. Nathan MACLIN and Martha Nickens. Married by Rev.
James Watkins. See Nathan Mackling. Ministers' Returns p 49

10 February 1790. Nathan MACKLING and Martha Nickins. Sur. Robert
Hill. See Nathan Maclin. p 19

2 November 1786. Philemon MAJORS and Elizabeth Chandler. Married by
Rev. Thomas Dobson. Ministers' Returns p 24

1 November 1786. Phillip MAJORS and Elizabeth Chandler, dau. W. W.
Chandler. Sur. Willliam Terry. Wit. William Chandler. See
Philemon Majors. p 8

1 May 1784. Daniel MALONE and Elizabeth Whitlock. Sur. Gruald Walling-
ham. Wit. Henry Goare. p 6

22 July 1785. Thomas MALONE and Susannah Tuck, dau. Thomas Tuck who
consents. Sur. David Powell. Wit. Robert Holt and Thomas Tuck, Jr.
Married 28 July by Rev. Thomas Dobson. p 7

- October 1772. Josiah MAN and Milley _____ek. Sur. William Wright.
Wit. Thomas Tunstall. p 3

25 April 1796. John MANN and Letty Sims. Sur. William Mann. p 34

15 March 1792. Robert MANN and Rebeckah Bass, dau. Henry Bass who
consents. Consent of Philemon Hurt, guardian of Robert Mann. Sur.
Stith Harrison. p 26

15 June 1781. Nathaniel MANNIN and Rebecca Watkins. Sur. George Watkins.
Wit. Henry Goare. p 5

29 June 1789. John MARSHALL and Patience Mann. Philemon Hurt, guardian
of Patience consents. Sur. William Mann. Wit. M. Hurt. p 17

10 May 1791. Thomas MARKELL and Betty Ashlock. Sur. Thomas Brown.
Consent of John Ashlock for Betty; no relationship stated. See Thomas
Mashell. p 23

12 November 1798. Matthew MARKHAM and Sally Jackson, dau. John Jackson
who consents. Sur. Edmund Chisum. Wit. Mason Murphy. p 39

23 November 1793. Austin MARTIN and Elizabeth Carr, dau. Thomas Carr who
consents. Sur. John Martin. Wit. Richard Johnson. Married
28 November by Rev. Hawkins Landrum. p 26

28 December 1795. Frederick MARTIN and Elizabeth Brown, dau. Frederick
Brown who consents. Sur. Jesse Puckett. Married by Rev. John
Atkinson. p 33

22 December 1800. Ganaway MARTIN and Betsey Tucker. Sur. Henry Tucker.
p 43

25 July 1791. Isaac MARTIN and Elizabeth Gillington. Sur. Joel Cheatham.
Married by Rev. Jesse Owen. Returned 5 October. p 22

27 February 1797. Isaac MARTIN and Sally Francis. Sur. William Brumfield. Wit. Jacob Ammonett, Charles Winfree and Moza Adams. Sally
signs her own consent. p 37

26 November 1798. James B. MARTIN and Nanny Owen. Sur. David Owen and
Nathan Martin. p 39

26 February 1779. John MARTIN and Elizabeth Dickerson Terry, dau.
Nathaniel Terry. Sur. Byrd Wall. Wit. Joseph Terry and Nathaniel
Terry, Jr. p 4

23 November 1793. John MARTIN and Polley Rice, dau. James Rice who
consents. Sur. Austin Martin. Wit. William Piles. p 26

7 February 1794. Jonathan MARTIN and Tabitha Hutson. Sur. Edmund
Clowdis. Wit. John Martin. Tabitha signs her own consent. Married
20 February by Rev. Reuben Pickett who says Hudson. p 31

23 September 1799. Jonathan MARTIN and Nancy Carmical. Sur. John
Martin. Wit. John Carmical. Nancy signs her own consent. Married
26 September by Rev. James Watkins. p 41

22 November 1790. Joseph MARTIN and Betty Owen. Sur. Nathan Martin.
Wit. Joseph Owen and John Owen. Consent of David and Sarah Owen for
Betty; no relationship stated. p 19

17 January 1794. Moses MARTIN and Delphy Martin. Sur. Samuel Oasley (Easley?) Delphy signs her own consent. Married by Rev. Philemon Hurt. p 30

28 June 1796. Richard MARTIN and Mary Hunt. Sur. David Allen. Mary signs her own consent. Married 30 June by Rev. Alexander Hay. p 34

30 September 1793. William MARTIN and Delphy Clardy, dau. Michael Clardy who consents. Sur. William Guill. Married by Rev. Philemon Hurt. p 26

7 January 1797. William MARTIN and Mary Vaughan, dau. Thomas Vaughan who consents and is surety. Wit. Alexander Pruett. p 37

11 May 1791. Thomas MASHEL and Betty Ashlock. Married by Rev. Hawkins Landrum. See Thomas Markell. Ministers' Returns p 55

11 August 1798. Charles MASON and Ann Scurlock, dau. Thomas Scurlock who consents. Sur. Dudley Scurlock. Wit. Nimrod Farguson. p 39

23 April 1793. Ezekiel MATHEWS and Sarah Cumbo. Sur. Thomas Maskell. Sarah signs her own consent. p 26

24 October 1791. Peter MATHEWS and Lucy Banger. Sur. William P. Martin. (Colored people). Married 28 October by Rev. William P. Martin. p 22

20 July 1790. James MATTHEWS and Molly Combo, dau. Thomas Combo who consents. Sur. David Gowing. Married 29 July by Rev. Hawkins Landrum. p 19

23 April 1792. Joseph MATTHEWS and Susannah Burchfield. Sur. James Matthews. Consent of John Burchfield for Susannah; no relationship stated. Married 28 April by Rev. William Moore. p 23

26 October 1789. Beverley MAYS and Sarah Stubblefield. Sur. Obadiah Gent. Sarah signs her own consent. Married by Rev. William Moore who says Sally. p 16

30 August 1784. Christian MAYS and Elizabeth Ragan. Married by Rev. Nathaniel Hall. Ministers' Returns p 7

7 September 1785. David MAYS and Frances Smith, dau. James Smith who consents. Sur. William Mays, Sr. Wit. William Smith and Wranson Day. Married 8 September by Rev. Hawkins Landrum. p 7

23 December 1792. Drury MAYS and Nancy Douglass, sister of William Douglass who consents. Sur. John Douglass. p 24

6 January 1792. Jonas MEADOR and Lucy Echols, dau. Moses and Elizabeth Echols who consent. Sur. John Echols. Married by Rev. John Atkinson. p 24

29 January 1794. Henry MECLARNEY and Sally Holt. Sur. John Holt. Sally signs her own consent. Married 30 January by Rev. Leonard Baker who says Maclency. p 31

25 July 1790. Henry MEDLOCK and Kerenhappoch Sandford. Sur. Joseph Sandford. p 19

1 November 1781. John W. MICHAEL and Mary Irvine. Sur. Robert Thurman. Wit. Henry Goare. p 5

20 February 1782. Lewis MILAM and Mary Holt. Married by Rev. Nathaniel Hall. Ministers' Returns p 9

12 June 1786. Thomas MILAM and Elizabeth Tolbert. Sur. David Neale. Elizabeth signs her own consent. p 10

24 February 1794. Calep (Caleb) MILLER and Salley Alley, dau. Elizabeth Alley who consents. Sur. Jesse Posey. Wit. Nathaniel Williams. p 30

9 April 1787. Frederick MILLER and Frances Carter. Sur. Presley Carter. Frances signs her own consent. Married 12 April by Rev. James Watkins who says Mary Carter. p 12

23 October 1798. John MILLER and Catey Hall. Sur. Benjamin Hall. Married 1 November by Rev. Thomas Dobson. p 39

27 January 1788. Martin MILLER and Rebeckah Douglass, dau. Mary Douglass who consents. Sur. Archibald Douglass. Married 31 January by Rev. William P. Martin. p 14

27 May 1795. William MILLER and Nancy Dickson. Married by Rev. Hawkins Landrum. Ministers' Returns p 110

29 September 1795. William MILLER and Susanna McNicoll. Sur. Samuel Rodgers. Wit. William Rice. Susanna signs her own consent. p 31

27 January 1800. Jeremiah MILNER and Orpha Anderson, dau. Meads Anderson who consents. Sur. Harrison Akin. Wit. Aaron Hardwick. p 43

9 September 1795. Luke MILNER and Susannah Bush. Sur. Thomas Bush.
Mark Milner signed consent for his son Luke saying he was 21 years
of age "last April." Consent dated 8 April 1795. Married 16 September by Rev. Hawkins Landrum. p 33

23 September 1793. Richard MILNER and Susannah Whitehead. Sur. Nipper
Adams. Wit. William Thompson and Benjamin Dickson. Richard and
Susannah both sign their own consents. p 26

9 May 1782. Robert Dudley MILNER and Mary Dickson, dau. Benjamin Dickson. Sur. John Lacey. p 5

25 October 1790. Thomas MILNER and Fanny Guthery, dau. Francis Guthery
who consents. Sur. Nipper Adams. p 19

25 May 1795. William MILNER and Nancy Dickson. Sur. Daniel Easley.
Nancy signs her own consent. p 33

31 July 1784. John MINNS and Tabitha Richardson. Married by Rev.
Nathaniel Hall. Ministers' Returns p 204

10 January 1793. Henry MINTERE and Mary Salmon. Married by Rev. James
Watkins. Ministers' Returns p 78

2 February 1789. Harrison MONDAY and Nancy Hughes. Sur. John Hughes.
p 15

22 October 1798. Byrd MOORE and Frances Stanfield, dau. Masd Stanfield
who consents. Sur. Richard E. Booker. Wit. Thomas Lankford. Bond
signed Burgis Moore. Married by Rev. John Atkinson. p 39

2 December 1799. Francis MOORE and Wilmurth Irby. Sur. William Irby.
Consent of Harrison Irby for Wilmurth. She was dau. Harrison and
granddau. Anthony Irby, will 22 October 1797. Married 8 December
by Rev. Thomas Dobson. p 42

22 December 1797. John MOORE and Elizabeth Wood, dau. Thomas Wood who
consents. Sur. Jesse Posey. p 37

26 January 1789. Mack MOORE and Sally Thompson. Sur. Richard Smith.
See Maness Moore. p 15

10 March 1789. Maness MOORE and Sally Thompson. Married by Rev. William
Moore. See Mack Moore. Ministers' Returns p 43

10 October 1781. Reuben MOORE and Chloe Irby, dau. Anthony Irby. Sur.
William Irby. Wit. Henry Goare. p 5

20 June 1786. Rice MOORE and Elizabeth Madison, dau. Roger Madison.
Sur. Obadiah Hendrick. Married 25 June by Rev. Hawkins Landrum. p 8

11 July 1791. Thomas MOORE and Rachel Wyatt. Sur. William Wyatt.
Married 19 July by Rev. Reuben Pickett. p 22

11 September 1798. Thomas MOORE and Polley Baker. Sur. Nimrod Farguson.
Polley signs her own consent. p 38

6 June 1798. Moore MOOREFIELD and Ruthy Strange, dau. Julias Strange
who consents. Sur. John Moorefield. Wit. John Dunkley. See Mose
Morefield. p 38

17 May 1787. John MOREFIELD and Winney Bruce. Sur. John Bruce. p 12

8 June 1798. Mose MOREFIELD and Ritter Strange. Married by Rev. Leonard
Baker. See Moore Moorefield. Ministers' Returns p 133

22 December 1785. Wright MOREFIELD and Nancy Stevens. Married by Rev.
Thomas Dobson. See Wright Morehead. Ministers' Returns p 15

3 December 1785. Wright MOREHEAD and Nancy Stevens. Sur. Kennedy Hill.
Wit. Molly Stevens and William Peter Martin. See Wright Morefield.
p 7

27 October 1774. Haynes MORGAN and Mary Thompson. Sur. Thomas Tunstall.
Wit. Mary Tunstall. Mary was the dau. William and Rachel Thompson:
she is mentioned in his will 31 March 1780. p 3

10 August 1798. Thomas MORNING and Susanna Chumbley. Sur. Drury Mays.
Consent of Gracy Chumbley for Susanna; no relationship stated. p 39

18 May 1792. Richard MORRIS, Jr. and Letty Scates, dau. Elizabeth Land
who consents. Sur. Thomas Morris. Married 19 May by Rev. Hawkins
Landrum who says Seats. p 24

19 August 1797. Samuel MORRIS and Betsy Peterson. Sur. Cason Guttery.
Married 24 August by Rev. James Watkins. p 37

15 March 1791. Thomas MORRIS and Tabitha Scates. Sur. Joseph Scates.
p 22

5 February 1795. Thomas MORRIS and Agnes Salmon. Married by Rev. James
Watkins. Ministers' Returns p 106

20 December 1787. William MORRIS and Rebecca Dawson. Sur. Thomas Morris.
Wit. Thomas Watkins. Rebecca signs her own consent. p 12

25 November 1785. Joseph MORRISON and Margaret Raney. Sur. Asher Reaves. Wit. James Watkins. Margaret signs her own consent. p 7

17 August 1797. William MOSELEY and Ann Williams, dau. John Williams who consents. Sur. Coleman Williams. Wit. Frances Camp. p 37

24 July 1782. Joseph MOTLEY and Elizabeth Irby. Sur. Nimrod Farguson. Wit. Henry Goare. Elizabeth signs her own consent. p 5

5 November 1789. Abner MULLINS and Jeddida Hampton. Sur. Hona Hampton. p 15

26 November 1792. Joel MULLINS and Kittury Drinkard. Sur. Archibald Drinkard. Kittury signs her own consent. Married 29 November by Rev. Jesse Owen. p 24

10 November 1781. John MULLINS and Lucy Smith. Married by Rev. Thomas Dobson. Ministers' Returns p 204

17 May 1792. John MULLNIS and Nancy Gentry. Sur. Henry Polley. Nancy signs her own consent. Married 7 June by Rev. Jesse Owen. p 26

9 January 1782. William MULLINS and Elizabeth Right. Married by Rev. Nathaniel Hall. Ministers' Returns p 206

10 December 1798. William MULLINS, Jr. and Frankey Estes, dau. Bartlett Estes who consents. Sur. Aylett Buckner. Wit. Thomas Buckner, Richard Royal and Jesse Mullins. William Mullins, father of William Jr. of Lunenburg County. Married 11 December by Rev. Thomas Dobson. p 39

21 May 1798. Jesse MUNDAY and Rebeckah Bruce. Sur. John B. Bruce. Married 24 May by Rev. Leonard Baker. p 3

27 January 1800. Edward MURPHY and Nancy Richardson. Sur. Henry Burge. Wit. Francis Spalden. p 43

5 December 1792. Francis MURPHY and Mary King, dau. Edmund King who consents. Sur. William Beal. Married 6 December by Rev. Alexander Hay. p 24

7 December 1796. James MURPHY and Sally Ford. Sur. John Murphy. Married 9 December by Rev. Hawkins Landrum. p 34

11 June 1792. Jesse MURPHY and Ruth Shelton, dau. Jonah Shelton who consents. Sur. John Murphy. Married 14 June by Rev. Hawkins Landrum. p 23

21 December 1790. John MURPHY and Sally Brown. Sur. Martin Brown.
Sally signs her own consent. p 19

29 July 1800. John MURPHY and Mary Robertson. Sur. Josiah Robertson.
Married 7 August by Rev. Hawkins Landrum. p 43

22 July 1784. William MURPHY and Mildred Hickman. Married by Rev.
Nathaniel Hall. Ministers' Returns p 7

26 August 1799. William MURRAY and Mildred Gresham. Sur. Anthony
Gresham. Married by Rev. James Watkins. p 41

13 November 1798. Thomas NAISH and Betsey Talley, dau. Daniel Talley
who consents. Sur. George Perrin. Wit. Branch Talley. p 39

22 December 1797. William NAISH and Elizabeth Bentley. Sur. Nathan B.
Stegall. Married 25 December by Rev. Leonard Baker who says Nash.
p 36

NASH see NAISH

11 October 1797. William NASH and Tabitha Parker, dau. Frances Parker
who consents. Sur. Abraham Parker. Wit. Polley Parker. Married
17 October by Rev. Thomas Dobson. p 37

27 July 1785. George NAVELL and Sarah Foster. Married by Rev. Thomas
Dobson. This name may be Novell. Ministers' Returns p 13

25 January 1800. Simon NEAL and Nancy Royster. Sur. John Royster. p 43

28 October 1791. David NEELEY and Peggy Hancock. Sur. William Irby.
Peggy signs her own consent. Married 1 November by Rev. Hawkins
Landrum who says Nealey and Henwick. p 21

28 September 1790. Robert NEELY and Margarett Chissum. Sur. Robert
Smith. Signs her own consent as Margaret Chissum. Married
30 September by Rev. Hawkins Landrum. p 19

10 October 1799. William NEELY and Elizabeth Lawson. Sur. John Lawson.
Married by Rev. Hawkins Landrum. p 41

19 September 1798. George NELSON and Susannah Guinn. Sur. John
Crittenden. Married 25 September by Rev. Leonard Baker who says
Gwinn. p 39

24 October 1798. John NELSON and Sally Thomas. Sur. Henry Thomas, Jr.
Married 30 October by Rev. Thomas Dobson. p 39

1 December 1797. Jeremiah NICHOLS and Sarah Parker Owen, dau. Ambrose
and Sarah Owen who consent. Sur. Daniel Owen. Wit. Thomas Dodson.
Married 5 December by Rev. Thomas Dobson. p 37

29 October 1791. George NEWBILL and Betsy Essex. Sur. Alexander Bomar.
Married 4 November by Rev. Hawkins Landrum. p 22

28 July 1788. John NEWBILL and Frances Bottom, dau. Sarah Bottom who
consents. Sur. William Oliver. Wit. Reuben Harris. p 14

5 December 1790. John NEWELL and Elizabeth Collins, dau. William
Collins who consents. Sur. Joseph Harvell. p 19

21 August 1792. James NEWTON and Sarah Ferrell, dau. William Ferrell
who consents. Sur. James Ferrell. Married 23 August by Rev. Thomas
Dobson who says <u>Terrell</u>. p 25

16 November 1786. John NICHOLS and Mary Legrand. Sur. Josiah Cathiel.
Married 23 November by Rev. Thomas Dobson who says LeGrand. p 8

23 September 1799. John NICHOLS and Patsey Chandler. Sur. Thomas
Clarke. Wit. Robert Hurt. Consent of Henry Chandler for Patsey; no
relationship stated. p 41

20 May 1797. Julius NICHOLS and Rebecca Nichols, dau. David Nichols who
consents. Sur. John Rickman. Wit. Matty Nichols. Married by Rev.
Thomas Dobson. p 36

7 February 1798. Matthew NICHOLS and Lucy Nichols, dau. William Nichols
who consents. Sur. Julius Nichols. Married 20 February by Rev.
Thomas Dobson. p 39

29 April 1797. Robert NICHOLS and Gincey Purcell. Sur. William Purcell.
Gincey signs her own consent. p 35

5 September 1791. William NICHOLS and Susana Dobson, dau. Thomas
Dobson. Sur. John Rickmon. Married 8 September by Rev. Thomas
Dobson. p 22

15 May 1787. Garnett NOEL and Elizabeth Bell. Sur. David Bell. Wit.
Frances Bell. Elizabeth signs her own consent. p 12

25 May 1756. James NORRELL and Mary Spraggins, dau. William Spraggins
who is surety. p 1

20 May 1797. Harbard NUNNALLY and Judith Farmer, dau. Frederick Farmer
who consents. Sur. Barnard Farmer. p 35

21 November 1782. Edward NUNNALLY and Sarah Vaughan. Married by Rev. Nathaniel Hall. See Edward Nunnelee. Ministers' Returns p 206

21 November 1782. Edward NUNNALEE and Sarah Vaughan. Sur. Drury Vaughan. Wit. Henry Goare. p 6

20 November 1793. James OAKES and Betsy Le Grand. Sur. William Macentire. Married 21 November by Rev. Thomas Dobson who says Patsy. p 28

3 April 1793. Laban OAKES and Susannah McKenny. Sur. James McKenny. Susannah signs her own consent. Married 4 April by Rev. Thomas Dobson. p 26

19 November 1794. James OAKS and Patsy Owen. Married by Rev. Philemon Hurt. See Josias Oaks. Ministers' Returns p 101

19 November 1794. Josias OAKS and Patsey Owen. Sur. Hezekiah Oaks. Wit. James Owen, Sarah Owen, William Owen and Martain Correnton. Consent of Rebecca Oaks for Josias; no relationship stated. See James Oaks. p 30

8 December 1792. Leonard ODEN and Ruth Stuart. Sur. David Stuart. Married 20 December by Rev. Jesse Owen who says Steward. p 24

20 March 1779. James OLIVER and Henrietta Briton Murray. Sur. William Oliver. Signs her own consent as Briton Murry. p 4

23 December 1793. James OLIVER and Judith Blackwell. Sur. Andrew Torian. Judith signs her own consent. Married 24 December by Rev. Leonard Baker. p 26

24 September 1799. James OLIVER and Mary Arnold. Sur. Richard Jones. p 41

5 June 1798. Nickerson OLIVER and Ann Richardson. Sur. William Chambers. Wit. John Mitchell. Consent of John Wimbish, apparently for both. p 39

6 May 1800. Nicherson OLIVER and Judith Holt. Sur. Bedford Davenport. Married by Rev. Nathaniel Holloway who says Nicholas. p 45

13 July 1791. William OLIVER and Vicey Johnston. Married by Rev. Thomas Dobson. Another copy of the Ministers' Returns says Lucy. Ministers' Returns p 52

25 September 1799. Enos ORGAN and Dicy Robertston, dau. Charles Robertson who consents. Sur. Christopher Robertson. p 41

2 November 1799. Edward ORSBORNE and Polly Osborn. Sur. Skeam Osborn. p 41

21 August 1795. Absalom OVERBEY and Lucy Thaxton. Sur. Logustin Pettypool. Consent of William Thaxton for Lucy; no relationship stated. Lucy Thaxton witnessed consent. Married 27 August by Rev. Reuben Pickett. From William Thaxton's will 1803 we find he mentions dau. Lucy Overbey. p 31

23 April 1792. Ahab OVERBEY and Sally Hughes. Sur. John Hughes. Sally signs her own consent. Married 3 May by Rev. Alexander Hay. p 24

5 December 1798. James OVERBY and Nancy Crowder, dau. Robert Crowder who consents. Sur. Samuel Woosley. Wit. William Craddock. p 39

25 July 1790. Shadrack OVERBY and Margaret Owen. Sur. Gregory Baynham. Margaret signs her own consent. p 19

8 February 1789. Joseph OVERTON and Mary Adams. Sur. Samuel Hubbard. Consent of John Adams for Mary; no relationship stated. p 16

23 December 1767. Abraham OWEN and Elizabeth Ray. Sur. Thomas Hope. Wit. Thomas Tunstall. This is out of place. Written 1776 and corrected 1767. p 3

26 October 1795. Barnett Bracket OWEN and Betsey Gutrey, dau. Travis Gutrey who consents. Sur. Ambrose Hart. Wit. Henry Barnes. p 31

10 August 1794. Champion OWEN and Judith Puckett, dau. Stephen Puckett who consents. Sur. Newbill Puckett. Wit. John Wood. Married 12 August by Rev. Thomas Dobson. p 30

12 October 1800. Daniel OWEN and Patsey Hudson, dau. Peter Hudson who consents. Sur. Sharod Owen. Wit. John B. Hudson. Married 14 October by Rev. Thomas Dobson. p 45

20 January 1794. Elijah OWEN and Nancy Lee, dau. William Lee who consents. Sur. Joseph Tuck. p 30

27 July 1781. Hatcher OWEN and Elizabeth Roberts. Sur. Benjamin Hall. Wit. Henry Goare. Signs her own consent as Betsy Roberts. p 5

10 October 1787. Hatcher OWEN and Mary Abbott, dau. Joseph Abbott who consents. Sur. Richard Abbott. Wit. Elizabeth Abbott and Frances Abbott. Married 16 October by Rev. Hawkins Landrum. p 12

2 January 1792. James Baker OWEN and Polly Whitton. Sur. Nathan B.
Stegall. Polly signs her own consent. Married 3 January by Rev.
Thomas Dobson. p 25

15 October 1794. James OWEN and Rhoda Gray. Sur. Joseph Owen. Wit.
Joseph Martin. Consent of Anney Gray for Rhoda; no relationship
stated. Married by Rev. Philemon Hurt. p 30

19 February 1788. Jesse OWEN and Jenny Hardwick. Sur. William Parker.
Jenny signs her own consent. Married by Rev. John Atkinson. p 14

22 October 1798. Jesse OWEN and Sally Jackson. Sur. Ephraim Jackson.
p 39

25 December 1800. Jesse OWEN and Lucy Bryan, dau. Elizabeth Bryan who
consents. Sur. Nelson Bryan. p 45

-    -   1794. John OWEN and Amey Lovelace. Married by Rev. John
Atkinson. Ministers' Returns p 98

22 November 1790. Joseph OWEN and Priscilla Tribble. Sur. John Owen.
Wit. Thomas Guthrea and David Owen. Peter Tribble consents for
Priscilla; no relationship stated. p 19

21 December 1788. Obadiah OWEN and Dicy Toombs. Sur. Champ Owen. Wit.
Thomas Dobson. Dicy signs her own consent. p 14

24 December 1790. Thomas OWEN and Mary Chandler. Sur. Peter Brown.
Wit. William Thompson. Signs her own consent as Maryann Chandler.
Married 30 December by Rev. Jesse Owen who says <u>Mary</u> <u>Ann</u>. p 18

3 December 1793. Thomas OWEN and Jane Roberts. Sur. Moses Roberts.
Married by Rev. Thomas Dodson. p 26

11 October 1797. Thomas OWEN and Nancy Hill, dau. William Hill who
consents. Sur. James Hill. Wit. Willis Chandler. Married
12 October by Rev. Hawkins Landrum. p 35

23 November 1790. Walter OWEN and Elizabeth Martin. Sur. Nathan Martin.
p 20

19 September 1795. Michael OZBROOK and Ruth Wilson. Sur. William
Wilson. Ruth signs her own consent. p 31

26 January 1795. Drury PALMER and Mary Faulkner, dau. Jacob Faulkner
who consents. Sur. William St. John. Wit. Benjamin Faulkner.
Married 28 January by Rev. Reuben Pickett. p 33

1 November 1791. Elijah PALMER and Ann Rebeckah Dobson, dau. Thomas Dobson. Sur. Jeffery Palmer. Married 2 November by Rev. Thomas Dobson. p 22

4 July 1782. Elisha PLAMER and Nancy Legrand, dau. John Legrand. Sur. Thomas Plamer. Wit. Henry Goare. p 6

16 March 1797. Isham PLAMER and Sally Johnson. Married by Rev. William Moore. See Isom Palmer. Ministers' Returns p 118

14 March 1797. Isom PALMER and Sally Johnson, dau. James Johnson who consents. Sur. Isaac Barr. See Isham Palmer. p 35

24 September 1791. John PALMER and Mary Jones. Sur. William Pride. Married 29 September by Rev. Thomas Dobson who says <u>John Thomas Palmer</u>. p 22

15 November 1798. Moses PALMER and Frankey Vaughan, dau. Drewry Vaughan who consents. Sur. John T. Palmer. Wit. Samuel Dunaway. p 38

10 May 1781. Daniel PALMORE and Elizabeth Nance. Married by Rev. Thomas Dobson. Ministers' Returns p 204

8 October 1766. John PANKEY and Betty Powell, dau. William Powell. Sur. Thomas Vaughan. Wit. John Cox and John Orvil Tunstall. p 2

29 October 1799. Abraham PARKER and Pheby Nichols, dau. Robert Nichols who consents and is surety. Wit. Jesse Nichols and John W. Nichols. Married 31 October by Rev. Thomas Dobson. p 41

15 March 1781. Daniel PARKER and Mary Anne Easley. Sur. William Parker. p 4

20 March 1799. Daniel PARKER and Betsy Lipscomb. Married by Rev. Thomas Dobson. Ministers' Returns p 139

6 September 1792. David PARKER and Sally Ginkins, dau. John Ginkins who consents. Sur. Lenord Abbott. Married 12 September by Rev. Thomas Dobson who says <u>Jenkins</u>. p 24

29 September 1794. John PARKER and Nancy Wood. Sur. Thomas Wood. Married 8 October by Rev. Hawkins Landrum. p 30

2 December 1794. Richard PARKER and Lucy Owen. Sur. John Owen. Married 4 December by Rev. Hawkins Landrum. p 30

31 January 1797. Richard PARKER and Polly Ligon. Sur. William Ligon. Married 2 February by Rev. Thomas Dobson. p 35

21 November 1792. William PARKER and Agge Henson, dau. Elizabeth Henson who consents. Sur. Littleberry Owen. Married 22 November by Rev. Thomas Dobson. p 23

1 January 1788. John PARKS and Patsy Church. Sur. Joseph Ligon. p 14

22 December 1789. James PARROTT and Katharine Parrott. Married by Rev. Reuben Pickett. Ministers' Returns p 47

6 December 1780. Lewis PARROTT and Sarah Scoggan. Sur. John Morefield. Wit. Henry Goare. p 4

25 August 1791. James PARTEN and Mary Eastis. Married by Rev. Reuben Pickett. See James Patten. Ministers' Returns p 54

6 March 1781. Thomas PASS, Jr. and Elizabeth Owen, dau. William Owen who is surety. Wit. Henry Goare. p 4

22 August 1791. James PATTEN and Mary Easter or Easte, dau. Thomas Easte. Sur. Simeon Glenn. See James Parten. p 21

29 October 1792. John PATTERSON and Bashe Butler. Sur. John Fourqurean. Wit. Edward Hall. Married 1 November by Rev. William P. Martin who says Barsheba. p 25

22 February 1791. Thomas PAYNE and Betsey Sowell. Sur. Irvine Christopher. Betsey signs her own consent. p 20

29 December 1798. Robert PAYNER and Sally Smith. Sur. John Stansfield who states Sally has no parents or guardian and has made her home with his family for 4 or 5 years. She is 22 years of age. Married 1 January 1799 by Rev. Nathaniel Holloway. p 39

24 September 1792. David PAYNOR and Catharine Mason. Sur. Richard Oliver. Married by Nathaniel Holloway. p 24

26 March 1792. Jesse PAYNOR and Eliza Oliver. Sur. Randolph Burkley. Consent of Richard Oliver for Elizabeth; no relationship stated. Married by Rev. Nathaniel Holloway who says Elizabeth. Returned 16 October. p 23

1 January 1797. John PEMBERTON and Elizabeth Fisher. Sur. John Fisher. p 35

24 December 1787. Michael PENDAR and Leticia O'Bryan. Sur. Charles Hoyle. Married 30 December by Rev. James Watkins who says Letty. p 12

3 November 1781. John PENDER and Ann Owen. Married by Rev. Nathaniel Hall. Ministers' Returns p 204

15 June 1797. William PENN and Margaret Martin. Married by Rev. Reuben Pickett. Ministers' Returns p 123

22 October 1798. Thomas PENTECOST and Mary Faulkner. Sur. John Faulkner. Married 25 October by Rev. Thomas Dobson. p 39

25 March 1793. John PENTICOST and Milley Fleming, dau. William Fleming who consents. Sur. Hillery Moseley. Wit. Henry Chandler and Coleman Williams. Married 2 April by Rev. Thomas Dobson. p 27

1 August 1789. Benjamin PERKINS and Dicey Hart. Sur. James Hart. p 16

22 August 1786. Joseph PERKINS and Sarah Brown. Sur. Richard Stanley. Married 7 September by Rev. Thomas Dobson. p 9

26 February 1798. George PERRIN and Salley Naish, dau. John Naish who consents. Sur. Moses Estes. Wit. Bartley Crowder. Married 27 February by Rev. Leonard Baker who says <u>Nash</u>. p 38

25 January 1790. Joseph PERRIN and Christiana Daniel. Consent of Terry Daniel for Christiana; no relationship stated. Sur. Royal Daniel. Married 6 February by Rev. James Watkins. p 17

24 December 1764. Samuel PERRIN and Jane Wade. Sur. Thomas Covington. Wit. Thomas Tunstall. p 1

24 December 1795. Stephen PETIPOOL and Milly Gregory. Married by Rev. Reuben Pickett. Ministers' Returns p 113

17 December 1789. John PHELPS and Lucy Walthall. Sur. Charles Old. Lucy signs her own consent. Married 24 December by Rev. Hawkins Landrum. p 15

8 November 1790. William PHELPS and Elizabeth McCraw. Sur. James McCraw. Married 11 November by Rev. Hawkins Landrum. p 20

22 February 1791. Richard PHILLIPS and Elizabeth Easley. Sur. Richard Finch. Married 23 February by Rev. Hawkins Landrum. p 21

22 September 1788. Ezekiel PILLER and Eleanor Martin. Sur. Nathan Martin. p 14

26 March 1792. James PINSON and Sarah Dupree. Sur. Joseph Glenn. Consent of Lewis Dupree for Sarah; no relationship stated. Married by Rev. Reuben Pickett who says Dupuy. Returned 19 April. p 23

7 October 1799. Chapman POINDEXTER and Betsey Johnson. Sur. John Johnson. Betsey signs her own consent. Married 10 October by Rev. Hawkins Landrum. p 41

23 December 1799. Joseph POINDEXTER and Frankey Harrison. Sur. John Marshall. p 41

23 March 1789. Thomas POINDEXTER and Susanna Keeling. Sur. Richard Parker. Married by Rev. William P. Martin. Returned 1 August. p 15

4 April 1789. Robert Petty POOL and Nancy Boyd. Sur. Robert Boyd. Married by Rev. James Watkins. p 15

24 September 1792. Henry POLLEY and Athaliel Mullins. Sur. John Lax. Consent of William Mullins for Athaliel; no relationship stated. Married 27 September by Rev. Jesse Owen. p 24

1 April 1795. John POLLEY and Mary Taler. Sur. Fortunatus Dodson. Wit. William Polley. Consent of Sarah Taler for Mary; no relationship stated. p 31

20 August 1794. William POLLEY and Sarah Haley. Sur. Fortunatus Dodson. Wit. Joseph Wood. Consent of Benjamin Haley for Sarah; no relation-ship stated. p 30

23 July 1792. John POOLE and Susanah Knight, dau. William Knight who consents. Sur. John Hewell. p 23

28 February 1797. Alexander POSEY and Elizabeth Stanfield, dau. Robert Stanfield. Sur. Jesse Posey. Wit. J. Stanfield and Nathan Buckley. Married 16 March by Rev. Nathaniel Holloway. p 37

3 December 1793. Benjamin POSEY and Susannah Easley, dau. Warham Easley who consents. Sur. Jesse Posey. Married 5 December by Rev. Hawkins Landrum. p 26

29 September 1798. Jesse POSEY and Susannah Wood, dau. George Wood who consents. Sur. Thomas Wood. Married 4 October by Rev. Hawkins Landrum. p 38

28 February 1791. Solomon POUND and Frances Bryant. Sur. John Thomas. Frances signs her own consent. p 21

23 November 1789. Anthony POWELL and Elizabeth Miller. Sur. Thomas Watkins. Married 51 December by Rev. James Watkins. Ministers' Returns p 40. p 17

15 December 1789. Anthony POWELL and Elizabeth Miller, dau. Elizabeth Miller who consents. Wit. John Gholson, Joseph Miller and Asher Reaves. This is consent only. Strange that it should be dated the day of the marriage and not the day of the bond. p 17

23 April 1794. Charles POWELL and Salley Nelson. Sur. John Nelson.
Married 24 April by Rev. Leonard Baker. p 30

17 January 1791. David POWELL, Jr. and Sarah Winn Smith Johnson. Sur.
Benjamin Hall. Wit. Robert Terry. Sarah dau. John and Susanna
Wooding. Step-dau. of John and dau. of Susanna. Married 18 January
by Rev. Alexander Hay. p 21

11 November 1796. David POWELL and Susannah Carter. Sur. Benjamin Hall.
Susannah signs her own consent. Married 17 November by Rev. James
Watkins. p 34

16 June 1788. James POWELL and Polly Turpin. Sur. Obadiah Turpin.
Polly signs her own consent. p 14

11 February 1800. James POWELL and Nancy Adams, dau. Will Adams who
consents. Sur. Philip Adams. Wit. Obadiah Robets. Married
13 February by Rev. Reuben Pickett. p 45

2 June 1787. Joshua POWELL and Fanny Willingham. Sur. David Powell.
p 12

4 September 1792. Thomas POWELL and Nancy Womack, dau. Charles Womack
who consents. Sur. Enoch Farmer. Married 6 September by Rev.
Hawkins Landrum. p 24

16 September 1784. William POWELL and Sally Johnson. Sur. Smith
Johnson. Wit. Henry Goare. p 6

25 December 1798. William POWELL and Nancy Nelson. Sur. John Hodges.
Married 26 December by Rev. Leonard Baker. p 39

25 November 1793. James PRESTON and Judy Samson, dau. William Samson
who consents. Sur. Samuel Weakley. Wit. William Smith. p 27

10 March 1778. Michael PREWIT and Mary Thurston. Sur. Charles Simmons.
Wit. George Watkins. Mary signs her own consent. p 3

11 February 1782. Byrd PREWITT and Sarah Hurt. Married by Rev.
Nathaniel Hall. See Byrd Pruitt. Ministers' Returns p 10

PREWITT see PRUITT

27 October 1793. William PRICE and Darens Hancer. This marriage is in
the Ministers' Returns but no name is signed. See William Rice.
Ministers' Returns p 206

18 May 1786. Williamson PRICE and Susannah Booker. Sur. Robert
Rakestraw. Married 31 May by Rev. Thomas Johnson. p 8

25 June 1798. James PRIDDY and Elizabeth Hodges, dau. Thomas Hodges who consents and is surety. Wit. John Hodges. p 38

21 February 1782. Richard PRIDDY and Judith Forester, dau. R. S. Forester. Sur. Dudley Glass. Wit. Henry Goare. Married 7 March by Rev. Nathaniel Hall who says Judith Forrest. p 5

19 September 1791. Pechey PRINTLE and Mary Jones. This marriage is in the Ministers' Returns but no name is signed. Ministers' Returns p 206

15 January 1793. William PRINDLE and Barbara Cooky. Married by Rev. Jesse Owen. Ministers' Returns p 80

15 November 1785. Anthony PRUETT and Susanna Gholson, dau. Mary Gholson. Sur. Francis Petty. Wit. Dabney Gholson. p 7

9 February 1782. Byrd PRUITT and Sarah Hurt, dau. W _____ Hurt. Sur. Philamon Hurt. Wit. Henry Goare. See Byrd Prewitt. p 6

11 February 1794. David PUCKETT and Letes Dodson. Sur. Jesse Puckett. Wit. George Chelton. Letes signs her own consent. Married by Rev. John Atkinson who says Lettia. p 30

28 November 1796. David PUCKETT and Annie Dodson, dau. David Dodson who consents. Sur. Jesse Puckett. Married by Rev. John Atkinson. Return dated 24 June 1797. p 35

22 June 1795. Hardy PUCKETT and Lucy Chaney. Sur. Daniel Hill. Married 1 July by Rev. John Atkinson. p 31

27 August 1792. John PUCKETT and Dorcas Chaney. Sur. Ransdell Petty. Wit. Edward Hall. Dorcas signs her own consent. See Jonathan Puckett. p 25

27 August 1793. Jonathan PUCKETT and Darcus Chaney. Married by Rev. John Atkinson. See John Puckett. Ministers' Returns p 73

21 December 1791. Newbill PUCKETT and Nancy Wood. Sur. William Thompson. Married 22 December by Rev. Thomas Dobson. p 21

- October 1785. Thomas PUCKETT and Elizabeth Wood. Sur. John Wood. Elizabeth signs her own consent. p 8

2 August 1798. Thomas PUCKETT and Fanny Arnold. Sur. James Arnold. p 38

30 December 1797. Joseph PULLIAM and Agness Brandon, dau. Eleanor Brandon who consents. Sur. William Brandon. Married 4 January 1798 by Rev. Nathaniel Holloway. p 36

23 May 1791. James PURCELL and Mildred Hall. Sur. Daniel Roberts. Mildred signs her own consent. Married 16 June by Rev. Alexander Hay. p 21

12 December 1796. William PURCELL and Nancy Parker. Sur. Benjamin Hall. Wit. Miles Parker. Nancy signs her own consent. Married by Rev. Thomas Dobson. p 34

5 October 1795. Benjamin PURKINS and Polley Willard. Sur. Joseph Purkins. p 31

28 July 1800. Daniel PURKINS and Mary Smith. Sur. William Smith. p 44

16 December 1793. Christopher PURSAL and Terusadeck Owen. This is in the Ministers' Returns but not signed by a minister. Instead it is marked "Teste: George Carrington, Clerk." Could this name be meant for Purcell? Ministers' Returns p 99

24 October 1796. Gideon RAGLAND and Polley Farmer, dau. David Farmer who consents. Sur. Walter Ragland. Married 10 November by Rev. William Moore. p 35

26 December 1792. Reuben RAGLAND and Betty Farmer, dau. Henry and Sally Farmer who consent. Sur. James Ragland. p 23

22 December 1788. Thomas RAGLAND and Frances Glass. Sur. Dudley Glass. p 14

9 March 1796. Walker RAGLAND and Betsy Comer. Sur. Reuben Ragland, Jr. Betsy signs her own consent. Married 19 March by Rev. William Moore. p 33

24 December 1800. Benjamin RAGSDALE and Mildred Dismukes, dau. John Dismukes who consents. Sur. William Martin. Wit. Joseph Ligon. p 43

22 December 1796. Lewis RAGSDALE and Sally Isbell. Sur. Thomas Collins. Wit. Joseph Faulkner. Sally signs her own consent. Married 29 December by Rev. Reuben Pickett. p 33

22 April 1793. Robert RANSOM and Nancy Hardridge. Sur. James Hardridge. Married 2 May by Rev. Hawkins Landrum. p 28

15 July 1767. William RAWLINGS and Mary Magdalin Roberts, dau. Alexander Roberts. Sur. Robert Jones, Jr. p 1

1 March 1794. John RAWLINS and Elizabeth Terrell, dau. William Terrell who consents. Sur. Timothy Terrell. Married 6 March by Rev. Thomas Dobson. p 30

17 November 1789. Benjamin READ and Nancy Black. Sur. William Oliver. Wit. James Oliver and Phillip Vaughan. Nancy signs her own consent. Married by Rev. James Watkins. p 16

10 October 1799. Daniel REAVES and Nancy Dobson. Married by Rev. James Watkins. Ministers' Returns p 155

16 January 1800. Thomas REEKS and Patsey Hill. Sur. John Hill. See Thomas Rickies. p 42

10 July 1798. John REES and Ally Binny Hands, dau. Mary Hands who consents. Sur. John Seal. Wit. Spencer Carter. p 38

26 November 1787. Joseph REYNOLDS and Elizabeth Turner. Sur. Waller Brown. Wit. Stephen Stewart. Elizabeth signs her own consent. Married 27 November by Rev. James Watkins. p 11

3 December 1796. Elijah RICE and Letty Jones, dau. Stephen Jones who consents. Sur. Henry Stackes. p 33

17 March 1781. John RICE and Elizabeth Hundley. Sur. William Matthews. Wit. Henry Goare. p 5

30 August 1784. Joseph RICE and Mary Cheatham. Married by Rev. Nathaniel Hall. Ministers' Returns p 204

27 October 1793. William RICE and Dorcas Huces (?). This is in the Ministers' Returns by not signed by a minister. Instead it is marked "Teste: George Carrington, Clerk." See William Price. Ministers' Returns p 99

1 October 1798. William RICE and Ann Richardson. Sur. James Jones. Ann signs her own consent. p 38

8 January 1781. George RICHARDS and _____. This incomplete marriage is in the Ministers' Returns by no name is signed. Ministers' Returns p 210

28 June 1787. Daniel RICHARDSON and Martha Forrest, dau. Richard Forrest who consents. Sur. Thomas Black. Wit. William Oliver and John Royal. p 12

16 August 1797. Jesse RICHARDSON and Nancy Caldwell. Sur. William Richardson. Nancy signs her own consent. p 36

20 October 1785. Thomas RICHARDSON and Lucy Thompson. Sur. George Thompson. Wit. William Peter Martin. p 8

10 September 1789. William RICHARDSON and Elizabeth Carter, dau. Theodrick Carter who consents. Sur. Hartwell Carter. Married by Rev. John Atkinson. p 15

28 January 1800. Thomas RICKIES and Patsy Hill. Married by Rev. Alexander Hay. See Thomas Reeks. Ministers' Returns p 147

16 February 1786. Simon ROACH and Jane Allen. Sur. Joseph Holt. Wit. Elizabeth White and Hampton White. p 10

1 May 1758. Alexander ROBERTS and Martha Smith. Sur. Zacahariah Smith. Wit. James MacCraw and William Wright. p 1

6 October 1760. James ROBERTS, Jr. and Elizabeth Oakes. Sur. William Wright. Wit. William Murphy and Charles Faris. p 1

25 May 1791. John ROBERTS and Mary Simms. Sur. Nathaniel Mannin. Married by Rev. Thomas Dobson who says Sims. p 21

26 September 1792. Thomas ROBERTS and Diana Chandler. Sur. William Thompson. Diana signs her own consent. Married 28 September by Rev. Thomas Dobson. p 26

1 December 1800. Thomas ROBERTS and Betsy Lacy. Sur. Matthew Lacy. Married 3 December by Rev. Thomas Dobson. p 43

22 September 1789. William ROBERTS and Sally Ragland. Sur. James Eastham. Sally signs her own consent. p 16

10 May 1800. William ROBERTS and Mary Camp. Sur. Thomas Roberts. Married 21 May by Rev. Thomas Dobson. p 43

14 January 1795. John ROBERTSON and Frances Abbott. Sur. Stith Harrison. Frances signs her own consent. Married 15 January by Rev. Hawkins Landrum. p 31

25 March 1797. John ROBERTSON and Mildred Price. Sur. Tyer Robertson. Married by Rev. Reuben Pickett. p 36

18 October 1790. Pleasant ROBERTSON and Mary Harper, dau. George Harper who consents. Sur. James Wilkinson. p 20

24 September 1792. Richard ROBERTSON and Polly Carmical. Sur. William Bragg. p 23

1 February 1762. William ROBERTSON and Elizabeth Hunt. Sur. Andrew Wade, Jr. Wit. William Wright. p 1

10 December 1796. Thomas ROBINS and Nancey Hudson, dau. William Hudson who consents. Sur. Daniel Owen. Married 15 December by Rev. Thomas Dobson. p 33

22 November 1790. Abner RODDEN and Agnes Brandon. Sur. Irvin Brandon. Wit. Joseph Martin and John Owen. Rebecca Brandon consents for Agnes; no relationship stated. Married by Rev. Nathaniel Holloway. p 20

6 May 1786. John RODGERS and Temperance Echols, dau. John Echols who
consents and is surety. p 10

6 July 1789. Benjamin ROGERS and Nancy Hill. Sur. John Phelps. Wit.
Charles Irby and Robert Wooding. Nancy signs her own consent. p 16

14 April 1794. William ROGERS and Betsy Glenn, dau. Simeon Glenn who
consents. Sur. William Hall. Married 17 April by Rev. Reuben
Pickett. p 30

18 January 1781. Philip ROSE and Sarah Hopson, dau. Henry Hopson. Sur.
William Peter Martin. Wit. Henry Goare. p 5

15 September 1768. Charles ROYSTER and Elizabeth How. Sur. Armistead
Watlington. p 2

22 May 1788. Peter ROYSTER and Susannah Roruck. Sur. Luke Powell.
Wit. T. M. Petty. Susannah signs her own consent. p 14

17 December 1800. John RUDDER and Susannah Richardson. Sur. William H.
Hunt. Susannah signs her own consent. p 45

23 October 1793. Absalom RUSSELL and Elizabeth Gaines. Sur. Matthew
Bates. p 27

15 December 1792. Christopher RUSSELL and Jerusha Owen. Sur. John
Owen. p 23

22 December 1796. George RUSSELL and Margaret Walters. Married by Rev.
William Moore. Ministers' Returns p 117

27 November 1798. Thomas RUTLEDGE and Lucy Baldwin. Sur. John Rutledge.
Consent of James Baldwin for Lucy; no relationship stated. Married
28 November by Rev. Alexander Hay. p 38

4 January 1794. Henry SALMON and Sarah Wood. Sur. William Wood. Sarah
signs her own consent. Married 9 January by Rev. James Watkins. p 30

24 December 1798. Robert SALMON and Susanna Grant, dau. Burrell Grant
who consents. Sur. Charles Grant. Wit. James Hitt. Married by
Rev. Nathaniel Holloway. p 38

30 December 1795. Jesse SAMPSON and Betsey Tune, dau. Travane Tune who
consents. Sur. James Preston. Married 31 December by Rev. Hawkins
Landrum. p 31

29 January 1793. James SANDERS and Keeron Medlock. Sur. William Yancey.
Keeron signs her own consent. Married 14 February by Rev. Alexander
Hay who says Kenon. p 27

11 October 1765. Thomas SANDERS and Mary Poliam, dau. Joseph Poliam. Sur. Adam Sanders. Wit. John Cox, Thomas Farguson and William Dyer. p 1

29 October 1793. William SANDS and Polley Traylor. Sur. Thomas Traylor. Married 31 October by Rev. Reuben Pickett. p 28

4 February 1764. William SATTERWHITE and Milley Dunn, dau. Walters Dunn. Sur. James McKendree. Wit. Thomas Tunstall. p 1

5 April 1794. William SATTERWHITE and Patsey Crowder, dau. Jean Crowder who consents. Sur. Adam Foot. No Witnesses. Married 6 April by Rev. Hawkins Landrum. p 30

8 February 1787. Joseph SCATES and Nancy Bruce, dau. Michael Bruce. Sur. John Carrington. Wit. Edmund and Mary Carrington. See Joseph Seats. p 11

19 April 1787. William SCATES and Nancy Keeling. Sur. Thomas Skates. p 11

28 January 1799. Zebulon SCATES and Lettey Pettey. Sur. Davis Petty. Married 14 February by Rev. Thomas Dobson. p 41

17 September 1785. John B. SCOTT and Patsy Thompson. Sur. John Coleman. Wit. Nathaniel Cocke and James Eastham. William Thompson, guardian of Patsy, consents for her. p 8

2 May 1791. Thomas SEAMON and Frances Hughes. Sur. Charles Gee. Frances signs her own consent. p 22

12 -   1791. Champness SEAMORE and Nancy Coats. Sur. William Coats. p 21

12 November 1792. Claborn SEAMORE and Sally Keen. Sur. William Farmbrough. Sally signs her own consent. Married 15 November by Rev. Jesse Owen who says Clayborne. p 26

5 August 1789. Burgis SEAMORE and Dicy Hart. Sur. James Brown. p 16

29 December 1798. Nathan SEAT and Sarah W. Pryor. Sur. John H. Pryor. Married 3 January 1799 by Rev. Reuben Pickett. p 38

7 February 1787. Joseph SEATS and Nancy Bruce. Married by Rev. Thomas Dobson. See Joseph Scates. Ministers' Returns p 25

11 February 1799. Amos SEAY and Polley Major, dau. Philip Major who consents. Sur. Willlliam H. Major. Married 14 February by Rev. Leonard Baker. p 41

5 February 1789.   John SEAY and Sally McCarty, dau. Jared McCarty who consents. Sur. Peter Torian. Wit. Andrew Juniel and George Torian. p 16

29 November 1792. Elijah SEBLEY and Polly Clay. Married by Rev. Jesse Owen. Ministers' Returns p 80

22 January 1799. Ephraim SEEMSTER and Elizabeth Shelton Bryan. Sur. William Johnson. p 41

9 March 1791.   Thomas SEYMORE and Rody Sparrow. Sur. Peter _____. Married by Rev. Thomas Dobson. p 22

15 June 1798. Wilcomb SEYMORE and Sally Hodges. Sur. William Hodges. p 38

1 May 1770.   Roger SHACKELFORD and Druscilla Hendrick. Sur. George Evans. Wit. William Wright. p 2

29 December 1794. James SHAW and Sally Newbill, dau. George Newbill who consents. Sur. John Shaw. Wit. Alexander Bomar and William Bomar. p 30

7 December 1773. John SHAW and Milley Hill. Sur. William Shaw. Wit. Henry Goare. p 3

2 December 1796. Miner SHAW and Wilmoth Bomar. Sur. Ephraim Hill. Wilmoth signs her own consent. p 33

6 November 1780. Benjamin SHELTON and Rebecca Watlington. Sur. Harrison Irby. Wit. Henry Goare. p 4

18 December 1793. George SHELTON and Larcenee Combs. Married by Rev. John Atkinson. See George Chelton. Ministers' Returns p 90

18 August 1800. James SHELTON and Suckey Wall. Sur. Charles F. Wall. p 43

16 May 1797. Josiah SHELTON and Futhey Ford, dau. Henry Ford who consents. Sur. James Crenshaw. Married 25 May by Rev. Hawkins Landrum. p 36

27 May 1793. Mark SHELTON and Nancy Dobson. Married by Rev. John Atkinson. See Mark Chelton. Ministers' Returns p 90

13 August 1796. Hardridge SHERON and Nancy Minor, dau. Daniel Minor who consents. Sur. George Carrington. Wit. William Hamlett, Jr. and Littleberry Hamlet. Married 18 August by Rev. William Moore. p 33

22 October 1798. William SHIELDS and Nancy Farmer. Sur. Enoch Farmer. p 38

3 December 1795. John SHOTWELL and Salley Ridgeway, dau. James Ridgeway who consents. Sur. Thomas Shotwell. p 31

26 December 1791. Gabriel SIBLEY and Nancy Bryan. Sur. John Bryan. John and Elizabeth Bryan consent for Nancy; no relationship stated. Married 29 December by Rev. Jesse Owen. p 21

7 November 1794. Jonas SIKES and Dicey Scott, widow. Sur. Jacob Sikes. Wit. Joab Sikes and Fanny Scott. Dicey signs her own consent. Married 22 December by Rev. Nathan Holloway. p 30

28 November 1791. Amos SILEATH and Sarah Jefres. Sur. Francis M. Petty. Sarah signs her own consent. Also spelled Silwick. p 21

5 May 1791. Thomas SIMMONS and Frances Hughes. Married by Rev. James Watkins. Ministers' Returns p 51

16 July 1773. William SIMMS and Cuzzy East. Sur. Mathew Sims. Wit. Paul Carrington. p 3

22 December 1791. Jesse SIMPSON and Mary Griffin. Sur. John Organ. Mary signs her own consent. Married by Rev. Jesse Owen. p 20

14 March 1799. David SIMS and Betsy Clark. Married by Rev. Thomas Dobson. Ministers' Returns p 138

14 December 1796. Matthew SIMS and Polly Mann. Sur. George Camp. Wit. Joel Mann and F. W. Mann. John Marshall, guardian of Matthew Sims, consents. p 35

17 March 1794. Peter SINGLETON and Salley Daniel. Sur. Jeremiah Terry. Wit. Susy Owing. Salley signs her own consent. p 30

3 September 1800. Abraham SLATE and Lucy Gaines. Sur. Thomas Gaines. Lucy signs her own consent. Married by Rev. John Atkinson. p 44

27 September 1790. Samuel SLATE and Betsy Orbrooks. Sur. Bennett Shelton. Consent of William Harris. (For Betsy?) p 18

22 December 1796. William SLATE and Caroline Clark. Married by Rev. William Moore. Ministers' Returns p 118

24 March 1794. Daniel SLATON and Elizabeth Hardwick. This is in the Ministers' Returns by not signed by a minister. Instead it is marked "Teste: George Carrington, Clark." Ministers' Returns p 100

5 November 1799. Stokley SLAYDEN and Nancey Dodson, dau. Thomas Dodson who consents. Sur. Joseph Dodson. Wit. Obediah Slayden. p 41

28 March 1791. John SMALLMAN and Pattey Fitts. Sur. William Keen.
Pattey signs her own consent. Married 3 April by Rev. William P.
Martin. p 21

2 February 1788. William SMART and Elizabeth Parrott. Sur. Jesse
Spradling. Elizabeth signs her own consent. Married 5 March by Rev.
William P. Martin. p 13

6 December 1786. Henry SMITH and Mary Hammons. Sur. James Hammons.
Henry son of Robert and Sarah Smith who consent. Wit. John Taloe.
Married 7 December by Rev. Hawkins Landrum who says Hammond. p 10

29 November 1787. James SMITH and Caty Wosher. Sur. Samuel Irby.
Wit. Edward Irby and William Smith. Caty signs her own consent. p 11

13 January 1791. James SMITH and Mildred Turner. Married by Rev. James
Watkins. Ministers' Returns p 49

7 January 1792. James SMITH and Jane Hopson. Sur. John Wood. Consent
of Henry Hopson for Jane; no relationship stated. Married 11 January
by Rev. William Moore. p 25

9 April 1794. Joseph SMITH and Frances Eastham, dau. Robert Eastham who
consents. Sur. Micajah Cayce. Married 10 April by Rev. Thomas
Dobson. p 30

13 November 1790. Osbon Jefferous SMITH and Margaret Burchfield. Sur.
Peter Washer. Both sign their own consents. See Osborn J. Smith.
p 20

17 November 1790. Osborn J. SMITH and Mary Burchett. Married by Rev.
Hawkins Landrum. See Osbon Jefferous Smith. Ministers' Returns
p 65

24 March 1794. Reuben SMITH and Mary Hobson, dau. Joseph Hobson who
consents. Sur. John Wood. Wit. E. Hobson. Married 27 March by
Rev. Reuben Pickett. p 29

7 January 1793. Robert SMITH and Tempy Mathews. Sur. William Smith.
Married 9 January by Rev. Hawkins Landrum. p 28

25 May 1795. Samuel SMITH and Isbell Carel. Sur. Jesse Sampson. Wit.
Richard Luttrell. Isbell signs her own consent. Married 27 May by
Rev. Hawkins Landrum. p 31

28 February 1791. William SMITH and Brigett Loveless. Sur. Benjamin
Dickson. Brigett signs her own consent. Married 3 March by Rev.
William Moore who says Bridget. p 21

27 November 1792. William A. SMITH and Mary Moore, dau. Daniel and Polly Moore who consent. Sur. Henry Easley. p 25

7 January 1793. William SMITH and Rebecca Mathews. Sur. Robert Smith. Married 9 January by Rev. Hawkins Landrum. p 28

26 November 1793. William SMITH and Jenney Hall. Sur. Benjamin Smith. Jenney signs her own consent. p 28

10 January 1798. William SMITH and Frankey Farmer. Sur. William Fourqurean. Frankey signs her own consent. Married 11 January by Rev. Leonard Baker. p 38

1 October 1800. William SMITH and Elizabeth Vier. Sur. Lovell Poindexter. Wit. William Morris and Benajmin Smith. Elizabeth signs her own consent. p 44

27 December 1790. Benjamin SNEED and Felicia Oliver, dau. Nickerson Oliver who consents. Sur. Peter Thaxton. Written Nick. Oliver. Married by Rev. Nathaniel Holloway who says <u>Sneed</u>. p 18

25 December 1799. Henley SNEAD and Sarah Hunt. Sur. James Hunt. Consent of Benjamin HUNT for Sarah; no relationship stated. Married 26 December by Rev. Thomas Dobson. p 42

3 August 1792. William SOWELL and Nancy Rawton. Sur. Peter Stern. Nancy signs her own consent. Married by Rev. Jesse Owen. p 24

24 December 1798. Reuben SPARROW and Mary Sparrow. Sur. Thomas Sparrow. p 38

29 December 1794. William SPARROW and Elizabeth Shaw. Sur. John Shaw. p 30

27 January 1800. Francis SPAULDING and Leo Decea Hancock. Sur. Ramsey Booker. Wit. Elizabeth Page, Robert Page and Jacob Page. Leo Decea signs her own consent. p 44

10 January 1792. Frederick SPOOLMAN and Margaret Cooper. Married by Rev. Nathaniel Hall. Ministers' Returns p 9

30 August 1785. Obediah SPRADLIN and Lucy Creel. Sur. William Eckhols (Echols). Wit. Mary Dodson. Thomas Dodson, guardian of Lucy, consents. Married by Rev. Hawkins Landrum. p 7

12 January 1781. Jesse SPRADLING and Elizabeth Colquitt. Married by Rev. Nathaniel Hall. Ministers' Returns p 204

3 January 1761. Nathaniel SPRAGGINS and Tabitha Finch. Sur. Robert Hutchinson. Wit. Thomas Spraggins. p 1

20 July 1769. William SPRAGINS and Frances Lucas, dau. James Lucas. Sur. William Lucas. Wit. John Brumfield. The original bond says Spraggins. p 2

28 December 1787. William STAMPS and Mary Wall. Sur. Charles Wall. Married by Rev. John Atkinson. p 11

9 December 1795. Ambrose STANDLEY and Caty Grimes. Sur. Thomas Hall. Wit. John Roberts. Caty signs her own consent. p 31

23 December 1794. John STANDLEY and Fanny Askew. Sur. Thomas Standley. Wit. John Ligon. Fanny signs her own consent. p 30

25 November 1793. Richard STANDLEY and Dicey Covington, dau. Thomas Covington who consents and is surety. Wit. Thomas Covington, Jr. and Ambrose Standley. Married by Rev. Thomas Dobson. p 27

20 October 1789. Abraham STANFIELD and Mary Farley, dau. Hannah Farley who consents. Sur. George Wiley. Married 29 October by Rev. Reuben Pickett. p 17

28 July 1788. Marmaduke STANFIELD and Rachel Pride. Sur. George Wily. Rachel signs her own consent. p 14

28 April 1788. Robert STANFIELD and Milley Coates. Sur. Walker Harris. Wit. William Stanfield and Harrison Stanfield. Milley signs her own consent. Married by Rev. James Watkins who says Standfield. p 14

5 November 1799. Thomas STANFIELD and Polly Waddill, dau. William Waddill who consents. Wit. John Waddill. Consent looks like Holly. This is consent only. Married by Rev. John Atkinson. p 42

20 December 1791. William STANFIELD and Sarah Farley, dau. Hannah Farley who consents. Sur. Robert Stanfield. Wit. Robert Stanfield, Walker Harris and John Stanfield. Bond written Standfield but all signatures are Stanfield. p 21

15 September 1784. John STANLEY and Saphire Brown. Married by Rev. Nathaniel Hall. Ministers' Returns p 7

2 October 1795. William STEEL and Polley Fambrough. Sur. Robert Weakley. Married 4 October by Rev. Hawkins Landrum. p 32

26 October 1791. Nathan B. STEGALL and Nanny Jennett. Sur. Edward Morefield. Nanny signs her own consent. Married 6 November by Rev. Thomas Dobson. p 21

13 July 1791. William STEPHENS and Susanna Smallman. Sur. Peter Brown. Married by Rev. Thomas Dobson. p 21

29 October 1794. Robert STEVENS and Isabel Cannady, dau. William Cannady
who consents. Sur. John Butler. Wit. Joseph Ashley. Married
30 Octber by Rev. Thomas Dobson. p 30

STEWART see STUART

17 October 1786. Matthew STEWART and Elce Proctor. Married by Rev.
Thomas Dobson. Ministers' Returns p 24

9 December 1799. Henry STOKES and Michael Steuart Ligon. Sur. Elijah
Rice. Michael signs her own consent. p 41

9 June 1781. Silvanus STOKES and Druscilla Pulliam, dau. Joseph Pulliam.
Sur. Howard Cain. Wit. John Pulliam, Jane Allen Pulliam and Agnes
Allen Pulliam. p 4

19 April 1759. William STOKES and Sarah Wade. Sur. Robert Wade, Jr.
Wit. William Wright. p 1

26 May 1785. Eusebius STONE and Milly Grant. Married by Rev. Hawkins
Landrum. Ministers' Returns p 11

23 December 1788. John STONE and Sarah Grant, dau. Jasper Grant who
consents. Sur. Jonathan Stone. p 14

18 December 1800. John STONE, Jr. and Peggy Chisher. Sur. Baptist
Chisher. p 44

20 December 1790. Jonathan STONE and Seffereign Moore, dau. Elijah
and Nancy Moore who consent. Sur. Jesse Simpson. p 18

15 July 1769. Joshua STONE and Mary Hoskins, dau. William Hoskins.
Sur. Anthony Irby. Wit. Samuel Hoskins. p 2

25 January 1796. William STONE and Elizabeth Easley. Sur. Isaac
Easley. p 33

25 January 1800. William STONE and Rachel Moore. Sur. Henry Jordan.
Married 3 January by Rev. Reuben Pickett. p 44

25 December 1797. David STOVALL and Nancy Whitehead. Sur. Benjamin
Dickerson. Both David and Nancy sign their own consents. Married
26 December by Rev. Hawkins Landrum. p 37

25 January 1786. George STOVALL and Elizabeth Eatham, dau. Robert
Eastham. Sur. Barton Stovall. Wit. John Roberts and James Eastham.
Married 26 January by Rev. Thomas Dobson. p 8

8 December 1795. George STOVALL and Rebecca Whitehead. Sur. Richard
Miller. Wit. D. B. C. Clark and Ben Dickson, Sr. Both George and
Rebecca sign their own consents. Married 10 December by Rev. Hawkins
Landrum. p 31

25 May 1789. Bailey STRANGE and Sucky Terrell. Sur. William Terrell. Sucky signs her own consent. Married by Rev. John Atkinson. p 16

25 July 1791. Josiah STRANGE and Elizabeth Weaver. Sur. William Strange. Wit. Thomas Ligon. Elizabeth signs her own consent. Married by Rev. Thomas Dobson. p 21

26 January 1792. Charles STUART and Elenor Stuart. Sur. David Stuart. Elenor signs her own consent. Married 9 February by Rev. Hawkins Landrum who says Stewart. p 23

20 December 1781. David STUART and Rachael Stewart. Sur. John Stewart. Wit. Henry Goare. Married 21 December by Rev. Nathaniel Hall who says David Stewart. p 4

27 October 1788. Martin STUBBLEFIELD and Sally Moore, dau. James Moore who consents. Sur. James Rice. Married 30 October by Rev. John Atkinson. p 14

25 December 1786. John SULLINS and Frances Edwards. Sur. William Edwards. Married 31 December by Rev. John Atkinson. p 10

4 October 1785. Nathan SULLINS and Elizabeth Farmer (widow). Sur. Thomas Bonner. Wit. Henry Goare. Elizabeth signs her own consent. p 6

28 October 1797. Manoah SULLIVAN, Jr. and Polley Tucker. Sur. John Fountain. Wit. John Atkins. Manoah Sullivan, Sr. consents for Manoah, Jr. Polley signs her own consent. Married by Rev. John Atkinson. p 37

24 September 1798. Ralph SULLIVANT and Nancy Mitchell. Sur. Benjamin Mitchell. Wit. William Keen. Nancy signs her own consent. Married 16 October by Rev. Thomas Dobson. p 38

12 November 1792. Elias SUTHERLAIN and Nancy Murphy. Sur. Jesse Younger. Married 24 November by Rev. Jesse Owen who says Southerland. p 25

14 December 1797. John Pumphrey SWINNEY and Elizabeth Brooks. Sur. James Brooks. p 36

22 January 1795. William SWINNEY and Salley Wells. Sur. Reuben Wells. Wit. Abram Wells. Salley signs her own consent. Married 31 January by Rev. Hawkins Landrum. p 31

5 March 1791. James SWINNY and Patty Blackwell. This marriage is in the Ministers' Returns but no name is signed. Ministers' Returns p 206

3 April 1770. Epaphroditus SYDNOR and Alice Milner. Sur. John Milner.
Wit. William Wright. p 2

13 November 1794. Elisha TALER and Elizabeth Gates. Sur. John Cacey.
Wit. John Taler. Elizabeth signs her own consent. Married by Rev.
Hawkins Landrum. p 30

26 November 1798. Charles TALBERT and Faney Coleman. Sur. Robert
Weakley. Wit. Elizabeth Coleman. Faney signs her own consent. p 38

15 December 1787. Berriman TAYLOR and Nancy Grant, dau. Phathy Grant
who consents. Sur. James Grant. Wit. Jeremiah Pate and James Dial.
Married 17 December by Rev. James Watkins who says Berryman Taylor.
p 12

10 January 1793. David TAYLOR and Mary Payne. Sur. John Robertson.
Mary signs her own consent. p 27

5 May 1788. James TAYLOR and Mary Wooding, dau. Robert Wooding who
consents. Sur. Peter Green. p 13

21 July 1792. William TAYLOR and Nancy Collins. Sur. James Collins.
p 23

18 December 1798. Benjamin TERRELL and Elizabeth Hobson, dau. Joseph
Hobson who consents. Sur. John Douglass. Wit. Charlotte Hobson
Beaufort and Nicholas Hobson. p 39

5 December 1797. Jesse TERRELL and Nancy Strange. Sur. Julius Strange.
Married 7 December by Rev. John Ligon. p 36

"March Court Day" 1795. Jerry TERRY and Winney Holt. This is in the
Ministers' Returns but not signed by a minister. Ministers' Returns
p 107

20 July 1786. John TERRY and Alesey Dickey. Sur. Ransome Colquitt.
Alesey signs her own consent. p 9

2 November 1783. Joseph TERRY and Sarah Hill. Sur. George Camp. p 6

5 November 1787. Keeble TERRY and Sarah Terry. Sur. Berryman Green.
p 11

27 July 1790. Bryant THOMAS and Dolly Strange. Sur. Benjamin Strange.
Dolly signs her own consent. p 18

25 December 1792. Elijah THOMAS and Polly Owen. Sur. John Owen.
Married by Rev. Thomas Dobson. p 23

23 July 1798. Henry THOMAS and Lucy Nelson. Sur. George Nelson. Married 7 August by Rev. Leonard Baker. p 38

28 June 1792. Jacob THOMAS and Hannah Farley. Sur. John Farley. Hannah Farley, guardian of Hannah consents. p 23

4 September 1787. Joel THOMAS and Agness Owen, dau. William Owen who consents. Sur. Solamon Pounds. Wit. John Thomas. Married 6 September by Rev. Hawkins Landrum. p 12

25 November 1793. John THOMAS and Sally Younger, dau. William Younger who consents. Sur. Elijah Thomas. Married 4 December by Rev. Leonard Baker. p 27

30 December 1794. Obadiah THOMAS and Rebeckah Posey. Sur. Jesse Posey. Wit. Obadiah Kent. Rebeckah signs her own consent. p 30

11 August 1781. Robert THOMAS and Sarah Lawson. Sur. William Lawson. Wit. Henry Goare. p 5

30 June 1794. William THOMAS and Frances Crowder. Sur. George Thomas. Wit. John Combe. Frances signs her own consent. Married 3 July by Rev. Alexander Hay. p 30

26 April 1786. James THOMPSON and Polly Terry. Sur. Nathaniel Terry. Polly signs her own consent. p 9

12 March 1793. John THOMPSON and Rebecca Scurlock. Sur. Thomas Scurlock. Married by Rev. John Atkinson. p 27

26 September 1793. John THOMPSON, Jr. and Rebecca Whitton. Sur. John Thompscn. Married 30 September by Rev. Leonard Baker who says Whitlow. p 28

15 November 1790. Joseph THOMPSON and Polly Forgerson. Sur. John Forgerson. Jane Forgerson consents for Polly; no relationship stated. Married by Rev. John Atkinson. p 18

17 November 1798. Joseph THOMPSON and Anna Owen. Sur. Thomas Lovelace. Wit. Charles Harris and William W. Womack. Anna signs her own consent. Married by Rev. John Atkinson. p 38

2 February 1789. Richard THOMPSON and Mary Moore. Sur. Edward Henderson. Married by Rev. William Moore. Returned 3 March. p 16

25 July 1787. William THOMPSON and Polly Watlington, dau. Armistead Watlington. Sur. John Watlington. She is mentioned in her father's will (1803) as Polly Terry. William Thompson died before 1803 and she married William Terry. She had three children by William Thompson: John, William, and Elizabeth. p 11

3 September 1800. James THORNTON and Jemima Seat. Sur. Nathan Seat. Jemima signs her own consent. Married 25 September by Rev. Reuben Pickett. p 44

15 December 1791. Julius THROCKMORTON and Rachael Cole. Sur. James Cole. Married 22 December by Rev. Thomas Dobson. p 22

8 April 1788. Robert THROCKMORTCN and Betty Hack. Sur. Julius Strange. Betty signs her own consent. p 13

9 January 1788. William THROCKMORTON and Nancy Nash. Consent of William Nash for Nancy; no relationship stated. Sur. John Dunkley. p 13

12 November 1792. Thomas THWEATT and Susannah Barksdale. Sur. James Eastham. Susannah signs her own consent. Married 15 November by Rev. Alexander Hay. p 24

31 December 1792. Thomas TINDALL and Patsy Wade. Married by Rev. Hawkins Landrum. Ministers' Returns p 92

29 January 1770. William TODD and Phoebe Farguson, dau. R. Farguson. Sur. Jeremiah Kern. Wit. John Wood and Joseph Abbot. p 2

26 October 1787. Jesse TOLLER and Phillis Yates, dau. Francis and Ann Yates who consent. Sur. William Yates. Wit. Reuben Ragland and Henry Farmer. See Jesse Towler. p 10

13 September 1791. Emanuel TOMBS and Elizabeth Jenkins. Married by Rev. Thomas Dobson. See Emanuel Toombs. Ministers' Returns p 52

1 September 1789. James TOMPKINS and Polly Hurt, dau. Mary Hurt who consents. Sur. James Townes, Jr. p 15

13 September 1791. Emanuel TOOMBS and Elizabeth Jenkins. Married by Rev. Thomas Dobson. See Emanuel Tombs. Ministers' Returns p 206

6 March 1796. Adam TOOT and Sally King. Married by Rev. Thomas Dobson. Ministers' Returns p 121

1 February 1773. Andrew TORIAN and Sarah Comer. Sur. Thomas Comer. p 3

29 March 1785. Andrew TORIAN and Anne Blackwell. Sur. Moses Blackwell. p 7

24 November 1794. George TORIAN and Sarah Ragland. Sur. John Ragland. Married 6 December by Rev. Alexander Hay. p 30

23 November 1789. Peter TORIAN and Susanna Palmer, dau. Edward Palmer who consents. Sur. James Palmer. Married 1 December by Rev. Reuben Pickett. p 15

25 March 1800. Scare TORIAN and Polly (Mary) Wade, dau. Charles Wade who consents. Sur. Hampton Wade. Wit. Thomas Torian. Married 27 March by Rev. Reuben Pickett. p 45

17 January 1793. Thomas TORIAN and Polley Torian, dau. Peter Torain who consents. Thomas son of Andrew Torian who consents. Sur. George Torian. Wit. Philip Rowolete. (?) Married by Rev. Alexander Hay. p 27

"Since July" 1787. Jesse TOWLER and Phillis Yates. Married by Rev. John Atkinson. See Jesse Toller. Ministers' Returns p 27

29 July 1780. Joel TOWNES and Mary McPearson. Sur. Humphrey Brooks. Wit. Henry Goare. p 4

2 October 1777. Stephen TOWNES and Lucy Watkins. Sur. William Watkins. Wit. Henry Goare. p 3

14 August 1780. Thomas TOWNES and Sally Wade, dau. Stephen Wade. Sur. Robert Wooding. Wit. William Pride. p 4

22 September 1800. Jeremiah TRAMMELL and Mary Colquett. Sur. Robert Trannell. p 44

11 July 1786. Thomas TRAYLOR and Phoebe Fargison. Sur. James Watkins. Married 13 July by Rev. James Watkins. p 9

7 November 1791. Benjamin TRAYNHAM and Elizabeth Palmer. Sur. Jeffrey Palmer. Married 14 November by Rev. Thomas Dobson. p 21

26 December 1791. George TRIBBLE and Mary Owen. Sur. Joseph Owen. Consent of David Owen for Mary; no relationship stated. Married 5 January 1792 by Rev. Jesse Owen. p 22

4 May 1793. Peter TRIBBLE and Mary Pruitt, dau. Michael Pruitt who consents. Sur. James Tribble. p 27

28 November 1791. Martin TRUE and Mary Hill. Sur. Joseph Holt. Mary signs her own consent. Married 8 December by Rev. James Watkins. p 20

29 March 1790. Cary TUCK and Nancy Stanley. Sur. Marthew Lacy. Consent of John Stanley for Nancy; no relationship stated. Married 1 April by Rev. James Watkins. p 18

22 December 1791. Edward TUCK and Lucy Standley, dau. John and Silldar (or Sieldar) Standley who consent. Sur. James Weaver. Married 26 December by Rev. Thomas Dobson. p 20

4 November 1791. John TUCK and Eda Standley, dau. John Standley who
consents. Sur. William Thompson. Married 10 November by Rev.
Thomas Dobson. p 20

22 December 1790. Josiah TUCK and Tabitha Harris. Sur. Matthew Lacy.
p 18

22 August 1797. William TUCK and Hannah Irby, dau. Joshua Irby who
consents. Sur. Daniel Malone. p 36

3 December 1789. Elijah TUCKER and Betsy Bailey. Sur. John Bailey.
Wit. James Thompson. p 17

17 October 1799. Joel TUCKER and Usley Chappell. Married by Rev.
Hawkins Landrum. Ministers' Returns p 144

15 February 1796. James TUNE and Rebeckah Conley. Sur. Jeasey Samson.
Wit. Thomas Tune and John Bomar. Rebeckah signs her own consent.
Married 18 February by Rev. Hawkins Lnadrum. p 33

21   - 1786. Thomas TUNE and Milley King, dau. Rachel King who
consents. Wit. Henry King, John King and F. Tune. Sur. William
McDaniel. Wit. Martha McDaniel. p 10

29 December 1792. Edmund TURNER and Elizabeth Richardson, dau. John
Richardson who consents. Sur. William Clay. Wit. John D. Famer.
p 26

4 November 1799. George TURNER and Susannah Adams. Sur. Philip Adams.
Consent of John Adams for Susannah; no relationship stated. Married
7 November by Rev. Reuben Pickett. p 41

11 December 1797. Isham TURNER and Fanney Wall. Sur. Armistead Moore.
Fanney signs her own consent. p 37

17 February 1763. James TURNER and Mary McMahaney. Sur. William Wright.
Wit. John Cox. p 1

27 June 1779. James TURNER and Sarah Irby. Sur. Harrison Irby. Wit.
Henry Goare. Sarah signs her own consent. p 4

28 May 1788. John TURNER and Henrietta Johnson. Consent of Isaac
Johnson for Henrietta; no relationship stated. Sur. Matthew Bilbo.
Wit. Isham Turner. Married by Rev. Reuben Picket. Returns 2 July.
p 13

24 December 1798. Martin TURNER and Sally Stanfield. Sur. William
Stanfield. Sally signs her own consent. Married by Rev. Nathaniel
Holloway. p 38

6 February 1760. Meshack TURNER and Rebecca Roberson. Sur. Joseph
Bays. Wit. William Wright. p 1

28 November 1794. Stoakley TURNER and Susanna Vaughan, dau. William Vaughan who consents. Sur. Peter Barksdale. Wit. William Vaughan, Jr. and D. Vaughan. Married by Rev. Philemon Hurt. p 30

2 October 1798. William TURNER and Nancy Le Grand. Sur. James Vaughan who consents for Nancy as her guardian stating her father James Le Grand had removed from this county and state leaving her in his care. Married 9 October by Rev. Hawkins Landrum. p 41

12 November 1794. James TURPIN and Polley Smith, dau. James Smith who consents and is surety. Wit. James Powell. Married by Rev. Samuel D. Brame. p 29

27 February 1797. John TURPIN and Elizabeth Carter. Sur. Richard Carter. Married 8 March by Rev. Hawkins Landrum. p 36

30 December 1788. William TWEEDELL and Sarah Johnson, dau. Joseph Johnson who consents. Sur. Thomas Daniel. Wit. Ransom Colquitt, George Comb and Elizabeth Johnson. Married 1 January 1789 by Rev. John Atkinson. p 13

6 March 1800. George TWIDDEL and Betsey Williams, dau. Luke Williams who consents. Sur. John Chapman. Wit. Anthony Irby. p 45

- October 1788. Isaac TYNES and Mary Chatham, dau. Joel Chatham who consents and is surety. p 14

2 March 1791. George VASSER and Sally Hunt, dau. Eli Hunt who consents. Sur. Elijah Hunt. p 23

5 February 1799. Peter VASSAR and Polly Vassar. Married by Rev. Leonard Baker. Ministers' Returns p 134

8 December 1797. William VASSER and Tabitha White. Sur. Melchzedick Spraggins. Wit. E. Spraggins. Tabitha signs her own consent. p 36

6 February 1793. Chaney VAUGHAN and Elizabeth Martin, dau. William Martin who consents. Sur. John Martin. Wit. James McCraw. Married 7 February by Rev. Jesse Owen. p 27

5 February 1781. Frederick VAUGHAN and Nancy Boleware, dau. Sark and Nancy Boleware. Sur. Jesse Nichols. This name must be Boulware. p 4

15 December 1785. James VAUGHAN and Sarah Le Grand. Sur. John Williams. Wit. William P. Martin. Married by Rev. Thomas Johnson. p 8

15 February 1787.   John VAUGHAN and Anne Stanfield, dau. M. Stanfield
who consents.   Sur. George Wiley.   Wit. Jonas Chambers.   Married
2 March by Rev. James Watkins.   p 11

10 November 1798.   Peter VAUGHAN and Nancy Turner, dau. Martin Turner
who consents.   Sur. William Vaughan.   Wit. James Fuqua.   p 38

27 September 1790.   Philip VAUGHAN and Sarah Fleming Bates.   Sur. James
Bates.   Wit. Charles Bates.   Sarah signs her own consent.   p 18

11 August 1767.   Thomas VAUGHAN and Mary Moody.   Sur. Joseph Abbott.
Wit. William Todd.   p 2

9 December 1797.   Thomas VAUGHAN and Patsey Tucker, dau. Edmund Tucker
who consents.   Sur. William Martin, Jr.   Wit. Philip Carter and
William Martin.   p 36

20 December 1791.   William VAUGHAN and Lucy Le Grand, dau. James Le Grand
who consents.   Sur. James Vaughan.   Wit. John Dickie.   p 23

4 January 1774.   William VEICE and Martha Dodson.   Sur. Ephraim Hill.
Wit. Henry Goare and M_____ Carrington.   This is the Marriage
Register version.   See William Hill.   p 3

21 January 1790.   Paig VOWELL and Sarah Holt.   Married by Rev. James
Watkins.   Ministers' Returns   p 40

8 February 1795.   Page VOWEL and Nancy Parrot.   Married by Rev. James
Watkins.   Ministers' Returns   p 106

13 March 1800.   Moses WADDELL and Betsy W. Pleasants.   Sur. William
Keen.   Married 14 March by Rev. Drury Lacy.   p 44

30 June 1786.   Noel WADDILL and Elizabeth Carter, dau. Mary Carter who
consents.   Sur. William Waddill.   Wit. Nathaniel Waddill.   Married
by Rev. John Atkinson.   p 10

27 July 1770.   William WADDILL and Anne Carter.   Sur. John Carter.   Wit.
H. Gray.   p 2

11 March 1794.   Allen WADE and Polley Boxley.   Sur. William Boxley.
Benjamin Boxley consents for Polley; no relationship stated.   Married
13 March by Rev. Reuben Pickett.   p 29

22 November 1790.   Andrew WADE and Sarah Petty.   Sur. Francis M. Petty.
p 17

26 May 1798. Banister WADE and Patsey Terry. Sur. Spenser Carter.
Patsey signs her own consent. Married by Rev. John Atkinson. p 39

6 February 1761. Charles WADE and Isabell Boyd. Sur. John Armstrong.
p 1

31 October 1780. David WADE and Isabella Smith. Sur. John Gwinn.
Isabella signs her own consent. p 4

14 December 1785. Edmund WADE amd Tabitha Wyatt. Sur. Horatio Wade.
Wit. William P. Martin. Tabitha signs her own consents. p 8

14 December 1785. Horatio WADE and Sarah Wyatt. Sur. Edmund Wade. p 8

14 November 1793. John WADE and Patsey East, dau. Thomas and Agga East
who consent. Sur. Thomas Tuck. Wit. William White. Married by Rev.
Reuben Pickett. p 27

10 November 1785. Luke WADE and Martha Stanley, dau. John Stanley. Sur.
John Weaver. Wit. Robert Rickman, Robert Wade and Martha Stanley.
Married by Rev. Thomas Dobson. p 8

8 June 1786. Robert WADE and Sally (Sarah) Boyd, dau. George Boyd.
Sur. William LeGrand. Wit. Obadiah Hendrick. p 8

28 April 1790. Robert WADE and Sarah R. Vaughan. Sur. Nicholas Vaughan.
p 18

9 May 1798. Robert WADE and Elizabeth Bennett. Sur. Christopher White.
Wit. William Boxley. Elizabeth signs her own consent. p 39

25 August 1800. Robert WADE and Nancy Enroughty. Sur. Joseph Ligon.
Wit. James Ligon. Nancy signs her own consent. Married 11 September
by Rev. John Ligon. p 45

26 June 1772. Willliam WADE and Sarah Wade. Sur. Samuel Perrin. p 3

18 September 1792. William WADE and Patsy Booker, dau. John Booker who
consents. Sur. Robert Wade. Married 20 September by Rev. Thomas
Dobson. p 24

22 November 1791. John WAKEFIELD and Louisa Clark. Married by Rev.
Jesse Owen. Ministers' Returns p 57

16 January 1794. William WALDEN and Dulley Buckner. Sur. Owen Walden.
Dulley signs her own consent. Married 23 January by Rev. Hawkins
Landrum who says Dolly Burner. p 31

26 July 1800. John WALKER and Polley Turner. Sur. Richard Edwards. Polley signs her own consent. Married by Rev. James Watkins who says <u>Mary</u>. p 44

28 December 1789. Moses WALKER and Isbell Irvine. Sur. James Irvine. Married 31 December by Rev. Reuben Pickett who says <u>Isabell</u>. p 16

23 September 1793. Buckner WALL and Anne Whitton. Sur. Robert Wall. Wit. Robert Hamblett and William Hamblett. p 27

16 December 1762. Charles WALL and Elizabeth Bates. Sur. Richard Brown. Wit. _____ Lankford. p 1

14 August 1788. Charles WALL and Wilmuth Deuberry. Sur. Wallace Wilson. Wilmuth signs her own consent. p 13

16 August 1787. George WALL and Nancy Watlington. Sur. John Watlington. Nancy signs her own consent. p 11

19 January 1763. John WALL and Ursula Bates, dau. John Bates. Sur. Hamon Miller. p 1

26 December 1799. John WALL and Nancy Oliver. Married by Rev. James Watkins. Ministers' Returns p 155

24 December 1792. Parham WALL and Rachel Boyd. Sur. Pabruk (?) Boyd. Wit. George Boyd. Rachel signs her own consent. p 23

20 August 1785. Richard WALNE and Patty Phelps. Sur. John Phelps. Wit. William Peter Martin. Married 6 September by Rev. Hawkins Landrum. p 7

10 August 1790. Capt. John WALSH and Sarah De Graffenread. dau. Sarah De Graffenread who consents. Sur. Nicholas Hobson. Wit. B. Gilliam. p 17

11 March 1793. Archer WALTERS and Ida Slayton. This marriage is in the Ministers' Returns but no name is signed. Ministers' Returns p 206

22 November 1790. George WALTON and Delila Van Dike, dau. Sarah Chalmers who consents. Sur. William Walton. Called Delila Chalmers in mother's consent. Married 29 November by Rev. William Moore. p 18

24 February 1795. James WALTON and Elizabeth Goodman. Sur. William Walton. Wit. John Poindexter. Elizabeth signs her own consent. p 32

5 February 1793. Robert WALTON and Patty Bonner. Sur. John Henrick Firesheets. Wit. Reuben Ragland. Patty signs her own consent. p 27

1 November 1793. Robin H. WALTON and Drusilla Terry. Sur. William Walton. Drusilla signs her own consent. p 27

20 March 1797. William WALTON and Elizabeth Terry. Sur. William Moore. Wit. Robert Harris and James Walton. Elizabeth signs her own consent. Married 30 March by Rev. William Moore. p 36

19 April 1768. John WARD and Mary Smith, dau. James Smith. Sur. James Turner. Wit. James Turner, Sr. p 2

25 October 1796. Seth WARD and Peggy Cobbs, dau. Samuel Cobbs who consents. Sur. Robert Cobbs. Married 27 October by Rev. Charles Cobb who says Cobb. p 35

19 December 1797. William WARD and Salley Ward. Sur. Nathan Seat. Wit. Wiley Ward. Consent of Samuel and Salley Ward for Salley; no relationship stated. Married 24 December by Rev. James Watkins. p 36

18 October 1787. Hackley WARREN and Frances Turner. Sur. James Holt. Wit. Basil Turner. Frances signs her own consent. Married 2 November by Rev. James Watkins. p 10

15 December 1794. James Stuart WARREN and Catherine Brandon. Sur. William Brandon. Catherine signs her own consent. Married by Rev. Nathan Holloway. p 29

16 October 1798. James WARREN and Dolley Stanfield. Sur. Benjamin Stanfield. Wit. Nathaniel Guthrie. Dolley signs her own consent. p 38

25 August 1788. Nathaniel WARREN and Lucy Powell. Sur. Charles Powell. Groom's name spelled Warrin. Married 4 September by Rev. James Watkins. p 13

12 December 1786. Jeremiah WARRIN and Mary Stanfield. Sur. George Wiley. p 10

27 February 1792. Larkin WARRIN and Unicia Farley. Sur. James Warrin. p 25

30 December 1799. John WASHBORN and Betsey Jennet. Sur. John Jennet. p 41

12 March 1787. Elias WASHER and Judy Boman, dau. John Boman. Sur. James Ashlock. p 11

17 December 1788. Peter WASHER and Mary Smith. Sur. William Smith. Consent of Robert and Sarah Smith saying both are of age. Married 18 December by Rev. Hawkins Landrum. p 13

11 October 1764. Micajah WATKINS and Mary Boyd, dau. Margaret Armstrong. Sur. John Armstrong. Wit. George Boyd, Jr., Isabel Wade and John Sullins. John Armstrong m. Margaret Boyd (widow) 1 January 1759. Married by Rev. Alexander Gordon, Rector of Antrim Parish. p 1

13 April 1780. Thomas WATKINS and Mary Tuck. Sur. Thomas Tuck. Wit. Henry Goare. p 4

29 February 1792. Edward R. WATLINGTON and Nancy Boyd, dau. Mary Boyd who consents. Sur. William Patrick Boyd. Married 7 March by Rev. Alexander Hay. p 25

23 December 1781. John WATLINGTON and Elizabeth Allen. Sur. David Allen. Wit. Henry Goare. Nathaniel Hunt signs certificate. p 5

22 September 1800. Thomas WATLINGTON and Sally Haskins, dau. Thomas Haskins who consents. Sur. Creed Haskins. Wit. John Watlington. Married 25 September by Rev. Alexander Hay. p 44

30 September 1797. James WATSON and Jane Conner, dau. John Conner who consents. Sur. Richard Burge. Wit. William Burge. Married 31 December by Rev. Hawkins Landrum. p 36

7 February 1798. Peter WATSON and Elizabeth White. Sur. Elisha Spraggins. Elizabeth signs her own consent. Married 8 February by Rev. Leonard Baker. p 38

11 March 1793. Archer WATTERS and Edna Slayton. This is in the Ministers' Returns but not signed by a minister. Instead it is marked "Teste: George Carrington, Clerk." Ministers' Returns p 99

24 May 1792. John WATTS and Betsy Roberts. Sur. Paul Carrington and Isaac Coles. Married by Rev. Alexander Hay. p 24

28 May 1799. Joseph WATTS and Patsey Canaday, dau. William Canaday who consents. Sur. Robert Stevens. Wit. Thomas Dodson and Thomas Stevens. Patsey also signs the certificate. Married 29 May by Rev. Thomas Dobson. p 41

13 May 1795. William WATTS and Patty Lee. Sur. Elijah Harris. Wit. Peter Dix. William Lee consents for Patty; no relationship stated. p 31

25 March 1793. Robert WEAKLEY and Jane Fambrough. Sur. Samuel Weakley. Wit. Thomas Parker. Jane signs her own consent. p 27

12 June 1797. Samuel WEAKLEY and Sally Vaughan, dau. William Vaughan who consents. Sur. William Sydnor. Wit. John Elliot. p 36

22 December 1791. James WEAVER and Vashti Tuck. Sur. Edward Tuck. Married 26 December by Rev. Thomas Dobson. p 22

21 December 1789. John WEAVER and Martha Nichols. Sur. William Nichols. Martha signs her own consent. Married 24 December by Rev. James Watkins. p 16

19 March 1798. Freeman WELLS and Martha Combs, dau. Mary Combs who consents. Sur. Daniel Dejarnett. Wit. William Smith. p 39

13 March 1797. Reuben WELLS and Tabitha Martin. Sur. Jacob Martin. p 36

14 February 1786. John WESLEY and Agatha Powell, dau. Charles Powell who consents. Sur. Joseph Flippo. Wit. William Wesley and James Watkins. Married by Rev. James Watkins. p 10

22 September 1788. John WEST and Rachael Spencer. Sur. William Bragg. Married 2 October by Rev. Reuben Pickett. p 14

12 August 1790. John WEST and Sarah Degraffenread. Married by Rev. Reuben Pickett. Ministers' Returns p 61

- -   1786. Joseph WEST and Anne Lawson. Sur. David Brandon. Anne signs her own consent. p 10

21 July 1794. Miles WEST and Lucy Parker. Sur. William Parker. Married by Rev. Thomas Dobson. p 29

7 February 1789. Christopher WHITE and Martha Church. Sur. Thomas Ligon. Martha signs her own consent. Married 24 February by Rev. Henry Lester. p 17

1 March 1790. Elias WHITE and Nancy Flyn. Sur. Christopher White. Nancy signs her own consent. p 19

9 January 1767. Epaphroditus WHITE and Tabby Spragins, dau. Thomas Spragins. Sur. John Cox. Wit. Mary Spragins. p 2

5 December 1788. Hampton WHITE and Elizabeth Mullins. Sur. Elias White. Wit. John Flynn and Thomas Wright. Elizabeth signs her own consent. p 13

21 January 1794. John WHITE and Phebe Clark, dau. Phebe Clark who consents. Sur. Thomas Clarke. Married by Rev. Alexander Hay. p 29

19 March 1771. Rawley WHITE and Mariah Spragins, dau. Thomas Spragins. Sur. Epaphroditus White. Wit. Charles Gallaway. p 2

8 September 1792. Allen WHITEHEAD and Bridget Brown. Sur. Martin Brown. Married 13 September by Rev. Thomas Dobson. p 26

28 November 1788. Thomas WHITLOCK and Susannah Webb, dau. John Webb who consents. Sur. Abraham Echols. p 13

15 December 1792. Thomas WHITLOCK and Judith Carter. Sur. Theodrick Carter. Judith signs her own consent. Married by Rev. John Atkinson. p 26

7 December 1786. Henry WHITLOW and Judith Parker. Sur. John Blackwell. Married 21 December by Rev. Thomas Dobson who says Whittlow. p 9

13 October 1800. John Willis WHITEMORE and Mary Barnes. Sur. Nelson Barnes. Wit. M. Petty. p 45

15 April 1782. John WHITWORTH, Jr. and Sarah Cunningham, dau. Joseph Cunningham. Sur. Daniel Parker. Wit. William Parker. John son of John Whitworth, Sr. p 5

17 December 1787. John WHITWORTH and Elizabeth Worley. Sur. John Farguson. Elizabeth signs her own consent. Married 18 December by Rev. Hawkins Landrum. p 11

22 August 1799. Thomas WILBORN and Susanna Ligon. Married by Rev. John Ligon. Ministers' Returns p 136

8 August 1791. William WILBOURN and Hannah Shelton. Sur. Decker Owen. Francis and Elizabeth Shelton consent for Hannah; no relationship stated. Married by Rev. Thomas Dobson. p 22

22 July 1783. George WILCOX and Sarah Vaughan. Married by Rev. Nathaniel Hall. Ministers' Returns p 8

26 February 1798. James WILKERSON and Sarah Hambleton. Sur. John Clay. Wit. Joshua Clay. Sarah signs her own consent. p 39

10 September 1792. Anthony WILKINSON and Margaret Jones. Sur. John Smith. Margaret signs her own consent. Married 13 September by Rev. Alexander Hay. p 23

4 November 1794. Edward WILKINSON and Milley Bruce, dau. Michal Bruce who consents. Sur. Edward Powell. Wit. John Clark. Married 5 November by Rev. Hawkins Landrum. p 29

20 February 1793. Henry WILKINSON and Polly Bruce. Sur. James Bruce, Jr. Married 21 February by Rev. Thomas Dobson. p 27

18 September 1799. James WILLIAMS and Sally Crews. Married by Rev. Thomas Dobson. Ministers' Returns p 139

15 June 1795. Luke WILLIAMS and Mary Parr. Sur. Joseph Pettey. Wit. John Carter. Mary signs her own consent. Married by Rev. Samuel D. Brame. p 32

15 September 1785. Thomas Jasper WILLIAMS and Mary McCraw. Sur. James McCraw. Wit. William P. Martin. Married 22 September by Rev. Thomas Dobson who says <u>McGraw</u>. p 7

21 November 1755. William WILLIAMS and Lucy Terry. Sur. Joseph Terry. p 1

14 November 1791. William WILLIAMS and Dorothea Traynham. Sur. David Traynbam. Married 17 November by Rev. Reuben Pickett. p 20

17 March 1795. Zachariah WILLIAMS and Frances Hagood, dau. John Hagood who consents. Sur. Burwell Hagood. Wit. Henry Hagood. Married by Rev. Samuel D. Brame. p 32

10 January 1800. Zachariah WILLIAMS and Ursley McGregor, dau. John McGregor who consents. Sur. William McGregor. Wit. James Adams. p 44

18 July 1793. Jarrald WILLINGHAM and Rachel Boyd. Sur. Joshua Powell. Rachel signs her own consent. This name is spelled Jarrell in the will of his father Jarrell Willingham 6 October 1790. Married by Rev. Reuben Pickett who says <u>Jerrell</u>. p 27

13 January 1796. Jarrell WILLINGHAM and Nancey Roberts. Sur. Peter Roberts. p 33

17 May 1790. Jeremiah WILLINGHAM and Tabitha Powell. Sur. William Powell. Wit. Joshua Powell. Tabitha signs her own consent. p 18

12 December 1791. David WILLIS and Drucilla Bragg. Sur. Hugh Bragg. David and Drucilla both sign their own consents. Married by Rev. James Watkins. p 22

14 October 1790. James WILLS and Patsey Murphy, dau. William Murphy who consents. Sur. Francis Murphy. p 17

27 April 1793. James WILLIS and Polly Murphy. Sur. William David. Polly signs her own consent. Married by Rev. Hawkins Landrum. p 27

17 March 1762. John WILLS and Ann Boyd. Sur. Thomas Green. Wit. William Wright. p 1

18 August 1785. Isaac WILSON and Susanna Mathews. Married by Rev. Hawkins Landrum. Ministers' Returns p 11

12 February 1800. Matthew WILSON and Marcy Forrest, dau. Richard Forrest who consents. Sur. James Forrest. p 44

16 April 1787. Robert WILSON and Patience Combow (Cumbo). Sur. Robert Smith. Patience signs her own consent. Married by Rev. Hawkins Landrum who says Cumbo. p 11

27 April 1789. Robert WILSON and Sarah Talbot. Sur. Richard Walne. Sarah signs her own consent. Married by Rev. Hawkins Landrum. Returned 21 May. p 16

5 February 1787. William WILSON and Cate Jett Hardwick. Sur. John Hardwick. Wit. James Hardwick. Cate signs her own consent. Married 7 February by Rev. Hawkins Landrum. p 12

2 January 1796. William WILSON and Janne Griffin. Sur. Wyley James. Janne signs her own consent. Married 7 January by Rev. Reuben Pickett who says Jane. p 33

26 January 1789. James WIMBISH and Lucy Hunt. Consent of Eli Hunt for Lucy; no relationship stated. p 17

18 September 1766. John WIMBISH and Mary Brady, dau. Oliver Brady. Sur. Thomas Cobbs. Wit. Epaphroditus White and Richard White. p 2

22 August 1780. John WIMBISH, Jr. and Sarah McCraw. Sur. James McCraw. Wit. Henry Goare. p 4

12 December 1796. John WIMBISH and Nancy Williams. Sur. William Sydnor. p 34

6 December 1788. Adam WINDERS and Mary Douglass. Sur. Terry Daniel. Mary signs her own consent. Married by Rev. John Atkinson who says Adam Windows. p 13

29 July 1790. Ep. WINDERS and Fany Chambers. Married by Rev. Reuben Pickett. Ministers' Returns p 48

17 October 1785. Abraham WOMACK and Tabitha Henderson. Sur. Frederick Vaughan. Wit. Stephen Jones. Tabitha signs her own consent. Married 21 October by Rev. Thomas Dobson who says Tabitha Hudson. p 8

12 March 1790. Allen WOMACK and Sally Womack, dau. Charles Womack who consents. Sur. William W. Womack. Wit. Charles Waddill. Married by Rev. John Atkinson. p 17

17 October 1762. William WOMACK and Mary Allen, dau. James Allen. Sur. William Wright. Wit. John Cox. p 1

7 August 1792. William WOMACK and Mary Logan. Sur. John Wimbish. Mary signs her own consent. Married 15 August by Rev. Hawkins Landrum. p 26

22 February 1798. William W. WOMACK and Nancy Dismukes, dau. Elisha Dismukes who consents. Sur. John Dismukes. p 40

11 November 1793. Archer Smith WOOD and Sally Pettey. Sur. Joseph Pettey. p 27

13 December 1786. George WOOD and Molly Wood. Sur. Thomas Wood. Married 14 December by Rev. James Watkins who says Polly Wood. p 9

22 December 1788. John WOOD and Caroline Matilda Smith. Sur. James Smith. Married 25 December by Rev. Hawkins Landrum. p 13

4 June 1765. Stephen WOOD and Anne Smith, dau. Samuel Smith. Sur. Thomas Tunstall. Wit. Thomas Coobs, John Gregory and William Gannaway. p 1

20 December 1787. Jacob WOODALL and Rebeckah Coventon (Covington). Sur. John Woodall. William and Febey Owen consent for Rebeckah. p 11

25 January 1786. John WOODALL and Susannah Stovall. Sur. Bartholomew Stovall. Married 27 January by Rev. Thomas Dobson. p 10

8 September 1797. John WOODALL and Nancy Tums. Sur. Philip Rowlet. Nancy signs her own consent. Married 9 September by Rev. Thomas Dobson who says Tombs. p 37

12 February 1793. William WOODALL and Martha Tolbeird. Sur. William Owen. Wit. William Tomson, John Woodall and Thomas Dobson. Martha signs her own consent. Married 13 February by Rev. Thomas Dobson who says Talbert. p 27

24 November 1774. John WOODING and Sucky Hill, dau. Elizabeth Hill. Sur. James Hill. Wit. David Grant. p 3

3 February 1786. John WOODING and Susannah Johnson. Susannah signs her own consent. (Was Susanna Johnson a widow? In 1791 her dau. Sarah m. David Powell, Jr.). Married 29 February by Rev. Thomas Dobson. Sur. Daniel Carter. Wit. Smith Johnson. p 8

26 May 1794. John WOODSON and Nancy Pleasants. Sur. William Keen. Consent of Jesse Pleasants for Nancy; no relationship stated. p 31

23 February 1797. Samuel WOOSLEY and Pheby Bailey. Sur. Thomas Bailey. Pheby signs her own consent. p 37

18 April 1786. Thomas WOOSLEY and Dianna Tribble. Sur. William Woosley.
Wit. Thomas Woosley, Sr. and Benjamin Hubbard. p 10

23 May 1791. Benjamin WORD and Elizabeth Edwards, dau. Richard Edwards
who consents. Sur. Henry Easley. Married 2 June by Rev. James
Watkins. p 20

6 February 1796. Morris J. WORD and Luvenia Jones. Sur. James Jones.
Wit. Richard Jones. Luvenia signs her own consent. p 33

24 November 1800. Thomas WORD and Tabitha Trible. Sur. James Trible.
p 44

8 October 1780. Amos WORRELL and Lucy Whitlock. Sur. John Arnold. Wit.
Henry Goare. p 4

22 April 1795. Conque (Conquest) WYATT and Fanny Hunt. Sur. Wyatt
Haley. Wit. John Wyatt. Reuben Hunt consents for Fanny; no relationship stated. p 32

19 November 1785. James WYATT and Lucy Martin, dau. John Martin. Sur.
Warner Martin. Wit. William P. Martin. Married 30 November by Rev.
Hawkins Landrum. p 7

25 August 1790. James WYATT and Milly Compton. Sur. David Hamrick.
Milly signs her own consent. p 18

25 January 1790. John WYATT and Leah Younger, dau. William Younger who
consents. Sur. Joseph Hopson. Married by Rev. William Moore.
Returned 20 February. p 18

24 December 1792. Major WYATT and Jane Faulkner. Sur. Ralph Gresham.
Jane signs her own consent. Married 3 January 1793 by Rev. Reuben
Pickett. p 24

23 February 1787. Vincent WYATT and Elizabeth Simpson. Sur. John
Simpson. p 11

23 December 1791. William YANCEY and Nancy Sandford, dau. Keeren Sanford.
Sur. William Keen. Married by Rev. Alexander Hay who says Sanford.
Returned 30 January. p 22

29 August 1797. Wylie YANCEY and Judy Ligon. Sur. Joseph Ligon.
Married 20 September by Rev. Reuben Pickett who says Judith. p 35

28 June 1790. William YEATES and Nelly Trammell. Sur. John Trammell.
Married by Rev. William Moore. Returned 1 October. p 18

17 November 1800. William YEATS and Elizabeth Minor. Sur. Aley (Alex?) Hardin. p 45

28 December 1792. Evan YOUNG and Mary Cumbo. Sur. Charles Cumbo. Married by Rev. Hawkins Landrum. p 26

26 July 1791. Josiah YOUNG and Betsy Fearel. Sur. Jesse Boyd. Consent of James Fearel for Betsey; no relationship stated. See Josiah Younger. p 20

23 January 1783. Jesse YOUNGER and Temperance Brown. Married by Rev. Nathaniel Hall. Ministers' Returns p 10

7 December 1799. John YOUNGER and Polly Owen, dau. Richard Owen who consents. Sur. David Allen. Wit. Benjamin Traynham. Polly also sgins the certificate. Married 12 December by Rev. Thomas Dobson. p 41

6 December 1788. Joseph YOUNGER and Sally Brown, dau. John Brown who consents. Sur. Martin Brown. Wit. Samuel Younger and John Winn. p 13

18 October 1791. Josiah YOUNGER and Eliza Terrell. Married by Rev. William Moore. See Josiah Young. Ministers' Returns p 67

28 June 1790. Thomas YULAND and _____ _____. Sur. Dudley Glass. p 17

KIDD, (Continued)
Tillithey 37
KING,
Elizabeth 26
Martha 26
Mary 66
Milley 94
Rachel 6
Sally 92
Sarah 34
KNIGHT,
Susanna 75

LACEY - LACY,
Betsy 80
Kitty 36
Sally 54
LAMBKIN - LAMKIN,
Rachel 40
LAWSON,
Agnes 41
Anne 101
Betsey 12
Elizabeth (2) 51, 67
Hannah 27
Isabel 37
Sarah 91
LAYNE,
Juriah 40
LEAGUE,
Anne 19
LEATS,
June 14
LEE,
Catherine 52
Nancy 43, 70
Patty 100
LEGRAND - LE GRAND,
Betsy 69
Betty 17
Lucy 96
Mary 68
Nancy 72, 95
Sarah 95
LEWIS,
Apphia 3
LIGHT,
Tabitha 18
LIGON,
Judith - Judy 106
Michael Steuart 88
Polly 72
Susanna 102
LINK,
Ann 9
Fanny 39
Rachel 4
LIPSCOMB,
Betsy 72
Polly 15
LOGAN,
Mary 105
LONDON,
Keziah 25
LONG,
Elizabeth 50
Sally 7
LOVELACE,
Amey 71
Bridget 85
Elizabeth 22
Tabitha 43
LOWRY,
Mary 59
LUCAS,
Frances 87
LUKE,
Sarah 59
LUMKIN - LUMPKIN,
Ginsey 2
Mathey 59

MACKALESTER,
Betsy 58
MACKEY,
Lucretia Edy 49
MADDOX - MATTOX,
Rosamond 36
MADISON,
Elizabeth 64
Frances 21
MAJOR,
Polley 82
MALONE,
Mary 42, 51
Sally 38
MANN,
Margaret 19
Patience 60
Phoebe 50
Polly 84
MARSHALL - MASHELL,
Elizabeth 22
MARTIN,
Delphy 62
Eleanor 74
Elizabeth 71, 95
Frances 8, 33
Lucy 106
Margaret 33, 74
Mary 6
Nancy Anderson 57
Susanna 49, 55
Tabitha 101
MASE - MUSE?,
Elizabeth 20
MASON,
Catharine 73
Sally 46
MATHEWS,
Rebecca 86
Susanna 103
Tempy 85
MAYBURY,
Elizabeth 59
MAY - MAYS,
Lucy 9
Mary 20
MC ALESTER,
Betsy 58
MC CALESTER,
Elizabeth 31
MC CARTY,
Elizabeth 7
Mary 7, 56
Sally 22, 56, 83
MC CORMACK,
Patsey 53
MC CRAW - MC GRAW,
Elizabeth 74
Mary 103
Mildred 50
Sarah 104
MC DANIEL,
Catherine 30
MC FARLIN - MC FARLAND,
Elizabeth 28
Susannah 20
MC GREGOR - MC GRIGOR,
Elizabeth 1
Sally 41
Ursley 103
MC INTIRE,
Mary 41
MC KENNY - MC KINNEY,
Cresia 33
Susannah 69
MC MAHANEY,
Mary 94
MC NICOLL,
Susanna 63
MC PEARSON,
Mary 93

MEDCALF,
Ruth 31
MEDLEY,
Jane Towles 59
Jinney 4
Judy 21
Mary 49
Patsey 38
Polly 40
MEDLOCK,
Keeron - Kenon 81
MEGRIGS,
Susanna 29
MERIWETHER,
Elizabeth 56
MICKELBOROUGH,
Elizabeth 42
MILLER,
Anney 40
Elizabeth 55, (2) 75
Mary 11
MILLINER,
Peggy 6
MILNER,
Alice 90
MINOR,
Elizabeth 107
Nancy 83
MITCHELL,
Cuzza - Cuzakiah 3
Henrietta 47
Nancy 89
MONDAY,
Tabitha 29
MOODY,
Mary 96
MOORE,
Elizabeth 8
Mary 86, 91
Rachel 88
Sally 89
Sarah 30
Seffereign 88
MOREFIELD,
Elizabeth 15
MOREHEAD,
Sarah 16, 17
MORRIS,
Elizabeth 49
Nancy 56
Sarah 52
MOSELEY,
Elizabeth Osborne 53
MULLINS,
Athaliel 75
Elizabeth 101
Grace 17
Jenny 17
Martha 29
Mary Watts 55
Polly 26
MUNDAY,
Ann 48
MUNFORD - MUNTFORD,
Rebeckah 6
MURPHY,
Betsy 6
Frances 11
Nancy 89
Patsey 103
Peggy 8
Polly 103
Sally 27
Sistyry 56
MURRAY,
Henrietta Briton 69
MUSAIN,
Tabitha 12

NANCE,
Elizabeth 72

ROBERTSON, (Continued)
  Marian 7
  Mary 67
  Phoebe 32
ROGERS,
  Catey 5
  Polly 29
ROLINGS,
  Sally 51
RORUCK,
  Susannah 81
ROWLETT,
  Fanny 37
ROYALL,
  Susanna 20
ROYSTER,
  Nancy 67
RUNNALS - REYNOLS,
  Elizabeth 24

SALMON,
  Agnes 65
  Ann 11
  Mary 64
  Susanna 11
  Winifred 11
SAMSON,
  Elizabeth 24
  Judy 76
SANDFORD - SANFORD,
  Betsey 36
  Kerenhappoch 63
  Mary 47
  Nancy 106
SANDS,
  Fanny (2) 14
SAWYERS,
  Susannah 37
SCATES,
  Elizabeth 35
  Letty 65
  Martha 38
  Mary 41
  Nancy 19
  Tabitha 65
SCOGGAN,
  Sarah 73
SCOTT,
  Catherine 32
  Dicey 57, 84
SCURLOCK,
  Ann 62
  Judah 46
  Rebecca 91
SEAMANS,
  Nancy 37
SEAMORE,
  Nancy 36
SEAT,
  Jemima 92
SEEMSTER,
  Isbell 17
SHAW,
  Elizabeth 86
SHELTON,
  Alice 51
  Dorcas 49
  Hannah 102
  Patsey 24
  Ruth 66
  Winney 26
SIDNOR,
  Nancy 57
SIKES,
  Martha 14
SIMPSON,
  Elizabeth 106
SIMMS - SIMS,
  Aney 3
  Betsey 20
  Keziah 49
  Lettice 57

SIMMS - SIMS, (Continued)
  Letty 60
  Mary 80
  Nancy 25
  Priscilla 16
SINGLETON,
  Polley 12
SLAUGHTER,
  Judith 36
SLAYTON,
  Enda 100
  Ida 98
SMALLMAN,
  Mary 43
  Ruth 13
  Susanna 87
SMITH,
  Anne 105
  Caroline Matilda 105
  Elizabeth 16
  Frances 62
  Isabella 97
  Lucy 66
  Martha 80
  Mary 78 (2) 90
  Nancy 26, 29, 54
  Polley 95
  Sally 73
  Sarah Winn 76
SNEED,
  Melley 5
SNELSON,
  Jane 6
SOLOMON,
  Anny 12
SOWELL,
  Betsey 73
SPARROW,
  Mary 86
  Rody 83
SPENCE,
  Elizabeth 36
SPENCER,
  Rachael 101
SPRAGINS - SPRAGGINS,
  Elizabeth 35
  Mariah 101
  Mary 35, 68
  Tabby 101
STAMPS,
  Nancy 27
STANDLEY
  Eda 94
  Lucy 93
  Martha 97
  Nancy 93
STANFIELD,
  Anne 96
  Betsy 15
  Dolley 99
  Elizabeth 75
  Frances 64
  Mary 42, 99
  Sally 94
STEPHENS - STEVENS,
  Elizabeth 45
  Nancy (2) 65
  Polly 53
STEWART,
  Hannah 32
  Nancy 50
  Polley 31
  Rachel 89
STONE,
  Anne 58
  Charity 7
  Elizabeth 5
STOVALL,
  Sally 27
  Susannah 105
STREET,
  Anne 13

STREET, (Continued)
  Frances 5
STUART,
  Elenor 89
  Ruth 69
STRANGE,
  Dolly 90
  Nancy 90
  Ritter 65
  Ruthy 65
STUBBLEFIELD,
  Mary 22
  Sarah 62
SULLINS,
  Mary 32
  Sarah 4
SWINNY,
  Fanny 56
SYDNOR,
  Alice 54
  Elizabeth 59

TABOR,
  Rhoda 31
TALBOT,
  Sarah 104
TALER,
  Mary 75
TALLEY,
  Betsey 67
TAYLOR,
  Betsy 55
  Elizabeth 45, 46
  Sally 45
TENNEY,
  Prissey 24
TERRELL,
  Eliza 107
  Elizabeth 78
  Fanny 8
  Jemima 21
  Salley 32
  Sucky 89
TERRY,
  Drusilla 99
  Elizabeth 38, 99
  Elizabeth Dickerson 61
  Joanna 37
  Lucy 103
  Mary 29
  Nancy 38
  Patsey 97
  Polly 91
  Sarah 37, 90
TOLBERT - TOLBEIRD.
  Elizabeth 63
  Martha 105
TOMSON,
  Susanna Walker 23
TOMBS - TOOMBS,
  Dicy 71
  Nancy 105
TORIAN,
  Polley 54, 93
  Sally 9, 59
TOWNES,
  Alice 26
  Elizabeth 57
  Levenia 1
  Lucretia 2
  Nancy 27
  Sally 39
THAXTON,
  Betsey 52
  Lucy 70
  Martha 26
THOMAS,
  Sally 67
THOMPSON,
  Anne 9
  Lucy 79
  Mary 1, 65

www.ingramcontent.com/pod-product-compliance
Lightning Source LLC
Chambersburg PA
CBHW072146020426
42334CB00018B/1898